The Development of the USA 1930–2000

John Wright, Steve Waugh
Editor: R. Paul Evans

The Publishers would like to thank the following for permission to reproduce copyright material:

Photo credits
p.3 © Library of Congress, Prints & Photographs Division, FSA/OWI Collection, LC-USF33-020522-M2; **p.5** © Margaret Bourke-White/Time & Life Pictures/Getty Images; **p.7** © The Granger Collection, NYC/ TopFoto; **p.8** © AP/TopFoto; **p.9** © Bettmann/Corbis; **p.12** Private Collection/Peter Newark American Pictures/The Bridgeman Art Library; **p.15** *t* Courtesy of the Franklin D. Roosevelt Library website, version date 2009, *b* © Archive Photos/Getty Images; **p.19** © Punch Limited/TopFoto; **p.21** © Bettmann/ CORBIS; **p.22** © Bettmann/CORBIS; **p.23** © Bettmann/CORBIS; **p.26** Catechetical Guild; **p.29** By Permission of the Marcus Family/Library of Congress, Prints & Photographs Division, LC-USZ62-75138; **p.30** *l* © Library of Congress, Prints & Photographs Division, LC-USZ62-117124, *r* LBJ library photo by Yoichi Okamoto; **p.31** © Punch Limited/Topham; **p.34** A 1973 Herblock Cartoon, copyright by *The Herb Block Foundation*; **p.37** © Everett Collection/ Rex Features; **p.38** © Susan Steinkamp/CORBIS; **p.39** © Patsy Lynch/Rex Features; **p.45** © Mary Evans Picture Library 2010; **p.46** © Everett Collection/Rex Features; **p.48** © Everett Collection/Rex Features; **p.49** © © Bettmann/CORBIS; **p.50** © © Henry Diltz/CORBIS; **p.51** © Mitchell Gerber/CORBIS; **p.53** © Bettmann/CORBIS; **p.55** The U.S. National Archives, NWDNS-179-WP-1563; **p.56** © H. Armstrong Roberts/ CORBIS; **p.58** © AP/AP/Press Association Images; **p.60** © Bettmann/ CORBIS; **p.63** © AP/Press Association Images; **p.64** Library of Congress, Prints & Photographs Division, FSA/OWI Collection, LC-USF34- 017417-E; **p.65** © AP/AP/Press Association Images; **p.67** Library of Congress, Prints & Photographs Division, The National Photo Company Collection, LC-USZ62-59666; **p.68** Library of Congress, Prints & Photographs Division, FSA/OWI Collection, LC-DIG-fsa-8a10410; **p.71** The U.S. National Archives,111-SC-337901; **p.72** Library of Congress, Prints & Photographs Division, FSA/OWI Collection, LC-USW3-034282-C; **p.73** © Bettmann/ CORBIS; **p.77** © Bettmann/CORBIS; **p.79** © Bettmann/CORBIS; **p.81** © Holt Labor Library; **p.83** *both* © © Time & Life Pictures/Getty Images; **p.84** Jackson Daily News/Fred Blackwell/AP/Press Association Images; **p.86** © Everett Collection/ Rex Features; **p.87** AP/Press Association Images; **p.88** © Central Press/Getty Images; **p.90** © Bettmann/CORBIS; **p.92** © Flip Schulke/Corbis; **p.93** © Popperfoto/Getty Images; **p.94** *t* © Ted Streshinsky/Corbis *b* © David J. & Janice L. Frent Collection/Corbis; **p.99** © Bettmann/CORBIS; **p.101** © Bettmann/CORBIS; **p.103** © Win McNamee/Getty Images; **p.104** © Topham Picturepoint/Press Association Images; **p.105** © George Burns/AP/Press Association Images; **p.113** © AP/Press Association Images; **p.116** Illingworth, Daily Mail 16 Aug 1941, by permission of the National Library of Wales/© Solo Syndication; **p.119** US National Archives (80-G-16871); **p.120** CPhoM Robert F. Sargent/US Defense Department; **p.124** © Time & Life Pictures/ Getty Images; **p.126** Harry S. Truman Library; **p.130** © Hulton-Deutsch Collection/CORBIS; **p.132** © Bettmann/CORBIS; **p.135** © Punch Limited/ TopFoto; **p.141** © © AP/Press Association Images; **p.142** © TopFoto; **p.145** © Les Gibbard, reproduced with kind permission of Susannah Gibbard; **p.147** © Bettmann/CORBIS; **p.148** © Bettmann/CORBIS; **p.152** © Peter Heimsath/Rex Features; **p.153** © Reuters/Corbis; **p.157** © Sipa Press/ Rex Features; **p.158** © JOHN GAPS III/AP/Press Association Images.

Acknowledgements
p.9 Source B: A.E. McIntyre, quoted in J. Simkin from *Evidence and Empathy: America in the Twenties*, 1986; **p.10–11** Source A: Herbert Hoover, from *http://hoover.archives.gov*; **p.15** Source D: Franklin D. Roosevelt, from *www.mhric.org/fdr/chat3.html*; **p.22** WJEC specimen question paper; **p.37** Source A: Ronald Reagan, quoted in Harriet Ward, *World Powers* (1985); **p.40** Source B: Bill Clinton, from *http://www. historyplace.com/speeches/clinton.htm*; **p.82** Source C: Martin Luther King, MIA mass meeting, 5 December 1955; **p.87** Source B: Martin Luther King, 'Letter from Birmingham Jail', 16 April 1963; **p.88** Source D: Martin Luther King, 'I Have a Dream', 28 August 1963; **p.89** Source F: Martin Luther King, 'I've Been to the Mountaintop', 3 April 1968; **p.95** Source B: Black Panther Party, 'What We Want, What We Believe' – The Ten Point Program, October 1966, from *www.spartacus.schoolnet.co.uk*; **p.102** Source A: Joint Center for Political and Economic Studies, Table showing black elected officials in the USA, 1970–2000; **p.103** Source D: adapted from *U.S. Census Survey*, Weekly wages data 1970–2000; **p.106** Source F: Smokey Robinson, Tamla Motown wikipedia site; **p.131** Source C: George Kennan, *The Sources of Soviet Conduct* (1947); **p.140** Source A: Doug Ramsey, quoted in N. DeMarco, *Vietnam 1939–1975* (1998); **p.142** Source D: quoted in C. Culpin, *Making History* (1996); **p.156** Source A: BBC News, 'Remembering the Iran hostage crisis', 4 November 2004; **pp.160–1** WJEC specimen question paper.

Although every effort has been made to ensure that website addresses are correct at time of going to press, Hodder Education cannot be held responsible for the content of any website mentioned in this book. It is sometimes possible to find a relocated web page by typing in the address of the home page for a website in the URL window of your browser.

Hachette UK's policy is to use papers that are natural, renewable and recyclable products and made from wood grown in sustainable forests. The logging and manufacturing processes are expected to conform to the environmental regulations of the country of origin.

Orders: please contact Bookpoint Ltd, 130 Milton Park, Abingdon, Oxon OX14 4SB. Telephone: (44) 01235 827720. Fax: (44) 01235 400454. Lines are open 9.00–5.00, Monday to Saturday, with a 24–hour message answering service. Visit our website at www.hoddereducation.co.uk

© John Wright, Steve Waugh, R. Paul Evans 2011
First published in 2011 by
Hodder Education,
An Hachette UK Company
338 Euston Road
London NW1 3BH

Impression number	5
Year	2015 2014 2013

CONTENTS

INTRODUCTION

▶ About the Route A course

During this course you must study four units:

- A study in depth focusing on source evaluation (Unit 1).
- A study in depth focusing on key historical concepts (Unit 2).
- An outline study focusing on change over time (Unit 3).
- An investigation into an issue of historical debate or controversy (Unit 4).

These are assessed through three examination papers and one controlled assessment:

- For Unit 1 you have one hour and fifteen minutes to answer the set questions. You must answer all the questions on the paper.
- For Unit 2 you have one hour and fifteen minutes to answer the set questions. You must answer all the questions on the paper.
- For Unit 3 you have one hour and fifteen minutes to answer questions on the outline study you have studied.
- In the internal assessment (Unit 4) you have to complete two tasks under controlled conditions in the classroom.

▶ About the book

This book covers the Unit 3 outline study 'The Development of the USA, 1930–2000'. It is divided into three sections, each with three chapters.

Section A: Changing life in the USA, 1930–2000

- The main influences on American life between 1930–1945 including the effects of the Wall Street Crash, the New Deal and the impact of the Second World War.
- The main political and economic developments in the USA after 1945 including how life changed in the 1950s, McCarthyism, the New Frontier and the Great Society, the Watergate Scandal and the domestic changes of US Presidents since 1981.
- Social developments in the USA 1945–2000 including changes in popular culture and youth culture, the student movement and the changing role of women.

Section B: Changing attitudes to the race issue in the USA, 1930–2000

- Racial inequality 1930–45 as a result of the Great Depression, the New Deal and the Second World War.
- Developments in the 1950s and 1960s in education and transport, as well as the influence of key figures.
- Progress for black Americans since the 1960s in legislation and the development of black culture.

Section C: The USA and the wider world, 1930–2000

- Changes in US foreign policy 1930–45; more especially the move away from isolationism.
- US involvement in the origins and development of the Cold War in Europe and the wider world.
- The role of the USA in the search for world peace since 1970, especially détente, the efforts of Reagan and Gorbachev and US involvement in Iran, the Gulf War and Iraq.

Each chapter:

- contains activities – some develop the historical skills you will need, others are exam-style questions that give you the opportunity to practise exam skills. Exam-style questions are highlighted in blue
- gives step-by-step guidance, model answers and advice on how to answer particular question types in Unit 3.

▶ About Unit 3

The examination in Unit 3 is a test of:

- knowledge and understanding of the key developments in each of the three sections
- the ability to answer a range of skills questions and source questions.

The exam paper will include a mix of written and illustrative sources:

- written sources could include extracts from speeches, letters, biographies, autobiographies, memoirs, newspapers, modern history textbooks, the views of historians, or information from the internet

- illustrations could include photographs, posters, cartoons or paintings.

You have to answer the following types of questions which ask you to demonstrate different source evaluation and writing skills:

- Describe/outline – asking you to give a detailed description, usually of the key events in a period.
- Change or continuity – using two sources and your own knowledge in your explanation.
- Judgement – asking you to make a judgement about either a turning point or the importance or success of a particular event, movement or individual.

- Essay writing – asking you to outline the degree of change or lack of change across the period 1930–2000.

▶ The examination paper

Below and on page 4 is an example of the type of examination paper you will sit for Unit 3. You will have one hour 15 minutes to complete **two questions from Section A** (out of a choice of three) and **one question from Section B** (out of a choice of three). The maximum mark allocation is 55. You could try this paper for practice once you have finished the course.

Section A
(The question below is similar to one of the three questions that will appear in Section A, of which you have to answer two.)

1 This question is about the changing attitudes to the race issue in the USA between 1930 and 2000.
   (20 marks in total)

   (a) Describe the Black Power movement.
   (5 marks)

   > This is a **describe /outline** question which tests your understanding of a key feature through the selection of appropriate knowledge. For further guidance, see pages 41–42 and page 144.

   (b) Use Sources B and C and your own knowledge to explain why the treatment of black Americans on public transport had changed.
   (7 marks)

   > This is a **change or continuity** question which asks you to identify change or lack of change (continuity) and to use your own knowledge to help describe and explain this, placing each source into context. For further guidance, see pages 60–62 and pages 126–28.

   Source A A bus station in Durham, North Carolina in the early 1950s

Source B From an interview with James Peck, a black American who rode the first freedom bus in May 1961

I entered the white waiting room and approached the lunch counter. We were pushed outside into an alleyway and six men started swinging at me with fists and pipes. Within seconds, I was unconscious.

(c) How important was Martin Luther King to the civil rights movement?
    (8 marks)

> This is a **judgement** question which requires you to make a judgement about the importance or success of a particular event, movement, individual or turning point. For further guidance, see pages 75–76 and page 96.

Section B

Answer **one** question only from this section.
(15 marks in total)
Marks for spelling, punctuation and the accurate use of grammar are allocated to this question (12 + 3 marks)

Either:

2 What have been the most important factors that have changed lives in America between 1930 and 2000?
In your answer, you may wish to discuss the following:

> ● *the impact of the Second World War*
> ● *changes in popular culture*
> ● *presidential policies from the 1970s*
> *and any other relevant factors.*

Or:

3 What were the most important factors that brought about change in the lives of black Americans between 1930 and 2000?
In your answer, you may wish to discuss the following:

> ● *the impact of the Second World War*
> ● *the civil rights movement*
> ● *progress made by black Americans by 2000*
> *and any other relevant factors.*

> This is a **synoptic essay question** which is intended to cover the whole period you have studied. Your aim is to outline the degree of change or lack of change across the period 1930–2000. For further guidance, see pages 108–10.

Or:

4 What have been the most important factors that have brought about change in American foreign policy between 1930 and 2000?
In your answer, you may wish to discuss the following:

> ● *the impact of the Second World War*
> ● *the USA and the Cold War*
> ● *the search for peace since 1970*
> *and any other relevant factors.*

What were the main influences on American life between 1930 and 1945?

Source A A 1937 photograph of black people queuing for relief in front of a famous poster

WORLD'S HIGHEST STANDARD OF LIVING

There's no way like the American Way

The USA was badly affected by the Wall Street Crash of 1929. It led to the Great Depression in both the cities and the countryside, with millions out of work. The Republican President Herbert Hoover became increasingly unpopular as he appeared to do little to ease the effects of the Depression. He lost the 1932 presidential election to Roosevelt who introduced a **New Deal** to help those badly affected by the Depression. There was, however, opposition to the New Deal from a variety of groups and individuals, more especially the **Supreme Court**. The Second World War finally revived the economy and removed unemployment.

This chapter addresses the following issues:

● What was the impact of the Wall Street Crash?
● What were the 'Hoovervilles'?
● Who were the Bonus Marchers?
● How successfully did Hoover tackle the Depression?
● Why did Roosevelt win the 1932 presidential election?
● How successful was Roosevelt's New Deal?
● Why was there opposition to the New Deal?
● What impact did the Second World War have on the economy?

TASK

Study Source A. What does it suggest about the USA in the 1930s?

Examination guidance
Throughout this chapter you will be given the opportunity to practise different exam-style questions. At the end of this chapter you will be given an overview of Question 1 of the Unit 3 examination paper.

What was the impact of the Wall Street Crash?

During the 1920s, more and more Americans began to invest in shares and prices kept rising. In 1928, however, shares did not rise as much as in previous years. This led to less confidence in the market and a drop in share prices. When, in the autumn of 1929, some experts started to sell their shares heavily before their value fell even further, small investors panicked and rushed to sell their own shares.

The real panic selling began on 19 October 1929. Nearly 3.5 million shares were bought and sold and prices began to fall quickly. The following Thursday, 29 October, became known as 'Black Thursday' as nearly 13 million shares were traded and share prices collapsed. Thousands of investors lost millions of dollars and were ruined. This event became known as the Wall Street Crash – named after the street where the US stock market was based.

▶ Unemployment

The impact of the Wall Street Crash was quite spectacular. By the end of 1929, there were about 2.5 million unemployed in the USA. This figure increased dramatically during the years 1929–32 due to the collapse of the US economy and the drop in world trade. Many businesses closed due to the fall in demand for American consumer goods both at home and abroad.

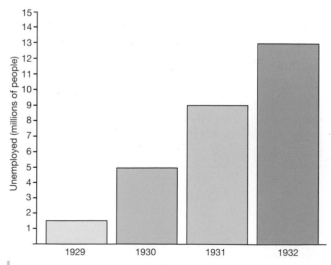

The growth of unemployment 1929–32

▶ Depression in the cities

Once the crisis began in October 1929, it was not long before factories began to close down. People stopped spending, and production had to slow down or stop. The industrial cities saw a rapid rise in unemployment and by 1933 almost one-third of the workforce was unemployed.

As people lost their jobs, they lost their homes. Some built alternative 'homes' in what became known as **Hoovervilles** (see page 8). Many of the unemployed in cities slept on the streets. Some drifted across the USA as **hobos**. They caught rides on freight trains in search of work. It was estimated that in 1932 there were more than 2 million hobos.

When the Depression began, black workers were often the first to be sacked. Their unemployment rate was 50 per cent by 1933.

▶ Depression in the countryside

Bankruptcy among farmers grew because they were unable to sell their produce. In many cases, food was left to rot in the ground. The drought of 1931 compounded the farmers' problems as reduced prices and falling output meant there was no hope of breaking even financially.

The states worst hit by the drought were Oklahoma, Colorado, New Mexico and Kansas. Poor farming methods had exhausted the soil, and in the drought the soil turned to dust. Therefore, when the winds came, there were dust storms. The affected area, about 20 million hectares, became known as the 'dust bowl'.

More than 1 million people left their homes to seek work in the fruit-growing areas of the west coast. Farmers and their families packed what they could, tied it to their cars or wagons, and set off towards the west coast. Those from Oklahoma were nicknamed 'Okies' and those from Arkansas were 'Arkies'. Farmers in the west were quite happy to employ these people as they worked for very low wages. They would set up camps at the edge of towns and seek work wherever they could get it. They were often resented by locals because they were taking their jobs.

Source A A photograph of hobos by a freight train, early 1930s

Source B From the memoir of Dorothea Lange, *The Assignment I'll Never Forget: Migrant Mothers*, 1960. Here she is describing meeting one of the migrant workers who had arrived in California

I approached the hungry woman ... She told me she was 32. She said she had been living on frozen vegetables from surrounding fields and birds that her children had killed. She had just sold the tyres from the car to buy food.

TASKS

1 Study Source A. What does it show you about the Depression in cities?

2 Explain why so many Americans migrated to the west coast during the early 1930s.

3 Was the Wall Street Crash a turning point in America's economic development? (For guidance on how to answer this type of question, see pages 75–76.)

▶ Family life

The Depression had a tremendous effect on family life.

● Young people were reluctant to take on the extra commitment of marriage. Marriages fell from 1.23 million in 1929 to 982,000 in 1932. The birth rate also fell.

● The suicide rate rose dramatically from 12.6 suicides per 1,000 people in 1926 to 17.4 per 1,000 at its peak in 1932.

● In some states, such as Arkansas, schools were closed down for ten months of the year because there was not enough money for teachers.

● The magazine *Fortune* estimated that by 1932 about 25 per cent of the population was receiving no income. Because there was no national system of social security, the unemployed and their dependants relied on charitable organisations such as the Red Cross.

What were the 'Hoovervilles'?

Source A A photograph of a 'Hooverville' in Seattle which existed from 1932–41

Those Americans who lost their homes as a result of becoming unemployed moved to the edges of towns and cities. They built homes of tin, wood and cardboard. These became known as 'Hoovervilles'. There was even a Hooverville in Central Park, New York. President Hoover was blamed for the lack of support and relief, and the sarcastic name for the dwellings soon caught on. It has been estimated that at their peak, several hundred thousand people across the USA lived in Hoovervilles.

Hoovervilles had no running water or sewage systems and thus caused public health problems for the towns and cities they were built in. There were frequent attempts to move the inhabitants but there were still Hoovervilles in existence as late as 1941, when the government put in place a policy to tear them down.

There were other terms, heavy with irony, which used Hoover's name:

- 'Hoover blankets' were layers of newspapers.
- 'Hoover flags' were men's trouser pockets turned inside out to show they had no money.
- 'Hoover wagons' were cars with horses tied to them because the owners could not afford petrol.

TASK

Describe living conditions in the Hoovervilles of the 1930s. (For guidance on how to answer this type of question, see pages 41–42.)

Who were the Bonus Marchers?

The Bonus Marchers were First World War veterans who had been promised a bonus for serving in the war, payable in 1945. The veterans felt that they could not wait that long to be paid. In May and June 1932, a Bonus Expeditionary Force, made up of over 12,000 unemployed and homeless veterans from all over the USA, marched to Washington DC to voice their support for a bill which would allow early payment of the bonuses.

The marchers brought their wives and children and built a Hooverville outside the capital and said they would stay there until the bonus bill was passed. Government officials labelled them a rabble. To pay the bonus to these men would have cost $2.3 million, and President Hoover felt that it was simply too much. **Congress** did provide money to pay for transport home for the marchers, but about 5,000 refused to leave. The government labelled these men communists and sent in the police to clear them from the old buildings they lived in. Conflict broke out and two veterans were killed.

Hoover then called in the army to control the situation. The armed forces were told to disperse the Bonus Marchers and the Hooverville was raised to the ground. More than 100 people were injured and a baby died of tear gas poisoning. This event left a bitter taste in the mouth of many Americans who were more convinced than ever that Hoover did not care.

Source B From an interview with A. E. McIntyre, Federal Trade Commissioner, who witnessed the attacks on the Bonus Marchers

The Bonus Marchers were very calm. When the army appeared the Marchers started beating on tin pans and shouting 'here come our buddies'. The Bonus Marchers expected the army to be in sympathy with them. Each soldier was in full battle dress. Each had a gas mask and tear gas bombs. Soon, almost everyone disappeared from view, because tear gas bombs exploded. Flames were coming up where the soldiers had set fire to the buildings in order to drive the Marchers out.

TASKS

1 Use Sources A and B and your own knowledge to describe how the Bonus Marchers were treated.

2 Working in pairs produce two different sets of headlines to accompany Source A:
- one by the government
- one by the Bonus Marchers.

Source A Soldiers driving the Bonus Army out of Washington DC with tear gas, July 1932

How did Hoover try to tackle the Depression?

Hoover won the 1928 presidential election and was president until March 1933. There is much controversy about Hoover's attempts to deal with the Depression. He was criticised at the time and in later years for doing too little to help those affected by the Depression. However, he did make some attempts to move towards recovery, especially in his later years as president.

▶ Hoover's early policies

Hoover has been criticised for allowing the economic situation to worsen after 1930. He was determined to **balance the budget** and refused to borrow money. He:

- kept faith with the Republican ideas of **laissez-faire** and '**rugged individualism**'. Rugged individualism was the belief that individuals are responsible for their own lives without help from anyone else, including the government. They should stand or fall by their own efforts

- met business leaders and asked them not to cut wages or production levels
- passed the Hawley-Smoot Tariff Act of 1930. This protected US farmers by increasing **import duties** on foreign goods. In retaliation, other countries refused to trade with the USA
- assisted farmers with the Agricultural Marketing Act of 1930. This act enabled the government to lend money to farmers through special marketing groups known as co-operatives which tried to fix reasonable price levels to ensure that goods were sold at a profit by farmers
- set up **relief agencies**, for example the President's Organisation for Unemployment Relief which aimed to promote and co-ordinate local relief efforts
- cut taxes by $130 million
- won approval from Congress for $1.8 billion for new construction and repairs to roads and dams across the USA.

Source A: A collection of statements made by Hoover when president. These statements were part of the Republican Party's ideas

A voluntary deed is infinitely more precious to our national ideal and spirit than a thousand deeds poured from the Treasury.

Each industry should assist its own employees.

Economic wounds must be healed by the producers and consumers themselves.

Each community and each state should assume full responsibility for the organisation of employment and the relief of distress.

Hoover's policies in 1932

However, with unemployment continuing to rise in 1931 and 1932, Hoover had to accept that his policies were not working. He obtained approval from Congress to introduce a series of other measures to relieve the crisis (see table below).

Measure	Description
Reconstruction Finance Corporation (February 1932)	Largest federal aid given – $2 billion in loans for ailing banks, insurance companies and railroads. To last only two years and would 'strengthen confidence' and stimulate industry and create jobs.
The Emergency Relief Act (ERA) (July 1932)	This gave $300 million to **state governments** to help the unemployed.
Home Loan Bank Act (July 1932)	This was to stimulate house building and home ownership. Twelve regional banks were set up with a fund of $125 million.

How successful were Hoover's policies?

Hoover's measures failed to pull the USA out of the Depression. He could not escape the fact that unemployment figures continued to rise. Many US citizens saw Hoover as callous and uncaring. The popular slogan of the time was 'In Hoover we trusted, now we are busted'.

On the other hand Hoover was not a total failure:

- He had persuaded state and local governments to expand their public works programmes and spending by $1.5 billion.
- He began to implement policies which were later followed by Roosevelt – such as helping banks and homeowners.
- During his four-year term of office federal spending on public works exceeded that of the previous thirty years. Some of the most important public works undertaken during this time included the San Francisco Bay Bridge, the Los Angeles Aqueduct and the Boulder Dam.

TASKS

1 Study Source A. What does it suggest about Hoover's policies towards the Depression?

2 Describe Hoover's early policies towards the Depression. (For guidance on how to answer this type of question, see pages 41–42.)

3 Study the three measures introduced by Hoover in 1932 (see table above). What was the purpose of each measure?

4 a) Draw a picture of some scales.
- On the left-hand side make notes on the success of Hoover in tackling the Depression.
- On the right-hand side note his failures.

Use your scales to help you answer the following question.

b) How successful was Hoover in dealing with the problems caused by the Depression in the years 1929–32? (For guidance on how to answer this type of question, see page 96.)

Why did Roosevelt win the 1932 presidential election?

Source A A Democratic election poster, 1932

Smile away the Depression!

Smile us into Prosperity!
wear a
SMILETTE!

This wonderful little gadget will
solve the problems of the Nation!

APPLY NOW AT YOUR CHAMBER OF COMMERCE
OR THE REPUBLICAN NATIONAL COMMITTEE

WARNING—Do not risk Federal arrest by looking glum!

In November 1932 a presidential election was fought between Hoover and Franklin D Roosevelt. Roosevelt won by a landslide – only six of the forty-eight states voted for Hoover. The result was 15,759,000 votes for Hoover and 22,810,000 for Roosevelt. Roosevelt's victory was due both to the unpopularity of Hoover and his policies and the appeal of Roosevelt and his promise of a New Deal, which the table below summarises.

TASKS

1 What is the message of Source A?

2 Design two posters for the 1932 presidential campaign, one for Hoover and one for Roosevelt.

3 Explain why Roosevelt won the presidential election of 1932.

Unpopularity of Hoover	Roosevelt's appeal
<ul><li>Hoover and the Republicans were blamed for the Depression.</li><li>They were blamed for failing to deal with the worst effects of the Depression.</li><li>It was only a few months since the harsh treatment of the Bonus Marchers.</li><li>Hoover had nothing new to promise voters.</li><li>Relief and government schemes were too small in scope.</li><li>Banks and businesses continued to fail and confidence fell away.</li></ul>	<ul><li>Many were impressed by the fact that Roosevelt had overcome the handicap of polio to become a successful politician.</li><li>Roosevelt created a mood of optimism to try to break the cycle of despondency.</li><li>At meetings he kept his message simple but offered a much bolder approach: *'I pledge you, I pledge myself, to a new deal for the American people.'*</li><li>This New Deal would include the creation of jobs, assistance for the unemployed and government help for both agriculture and industry.</li></ul>

What was Roosevelt's New Deal?

In his nomination speech Roosevelt had promised the American people a New Deal, and now that he was president it was time to deliver it.

After his inauguration, Roosevelt set to work immediately. He felt that it was his task to restore the faith that most Americans had lost in their country. The aims of the New Deal are set out in the table below and were based upon the 'three Rs' – Relief, Recovery and Reform:

Relief	• Assist in the removal of poverty. • Provide food for the starving. • Intervene to prevent people from losing homes/farms.
Recovery	• Ensure that the economy was boosted so that people could be given jobs.
Reform	• Ensure that there were welfare provisions in the future to help the unemployed, old, sick, disabled and the destitute.

The aims of the New Deal

Roosevelt attacked the problems of the Great Depression and pushed through a huge number of government programmes which aimed to restore the shattered economy. This period, from 9 March to 16 June 1933, became known as the Hundred Days. On 12 March 1933 he joked, 'I think this could be a good time for a beer'. The table on page 14 shows the most important of the Alphabet Agencies, the various organisations that Roosevelt set up during the Hundred Days.

The most important task waiting for Roosevelt at the beginning of the Hundred Days was to stem the crisis in banking. More than 2000 banks had closed in the twelve months before he had become president. He had to restore confidence in banking.

Roosevelt closed all banks for ten days and then, on the radio, with 60 million people listening, he explained his plans. He would allow those banks with assets to re-open and those without would be closed until he and his advisers put forward a rescue programme. He assured people that money was safer in the bank than at home. When the banks re-opened, people no longer wished to withdraw their savings. This radio talk became the first of many '**fireside chats**'.

Source A From *The Roosevelt I Knew* by Frances Perkins, 1946

When he broadcast I realised how clearly his mind focused on the people listening at the other end. As he talked his head would nod and his hands would move in simple, natural, comfortable gestures. His face would smile and light up as though he was actually sitting in the front porch or the kitchen with them. People felt this and it bound them to him with affection.

TASKS

1 Imagine you are the governor of a state which has industrial and agricultural workers. Write a letter to President Roosevelt indicating why his proposed solutions to the Depression will help these people.

2 Explain why Roosevelt's 'fireside chats' were so important. You may wish to refer to Source A for information.

3 Describe what happened during the Hundred Days. (For guidance on how to answer this type of question, see pages 41–42.)

The Alphabet Agencies

Agricultural Adjustment Act (AAA)	Set up to increase farm prices and farmers' incomes. To achieve this production levels would have to drop. As production fell, prices would rise and farmers would begin to recover. In other words, farmers would be paid by the government to produce less. More than 5 million pigs were killed and thousands of hectares of cotton were ploughed back into the ground. By 1936, incomes were one and a half times higher than they had been in 1933. The Supreme Court rejected the Act in 1936.
Civilian Conservation Corps (CCC)	Set up to create jobs for the many men aged between 18–25 who were hobos or living in Hoovervilles. They were offered work in conservation projects, such as planting trees to prevent soil erosion. They received food, clothing and one dollar per day. By August 1933 there were about 250,000 men in the CCC and by 1941 more than 2 million men had been granted some work with the CCC.
The Civil Works Administration (CWA)	Set up to create public jobs. By January 1934, about 4 million mainly unskilled Americans were on the CWA's payroll. Some of the workers built roads. However, some of the jobs were laughed at because they included scaring birds away from buildings or sweeping leaves in parks. In 1935 it was replaced by the Works Progress Administration (WPA).
Emergency Banking Act (EBA)	Set up to restore confidence in the banking system. Part of the Act prevented banks from investing savings deposits in the **stock market** which was too unpredictable to guarantee the safety of those funds.
Farm Credit Administration (FCA)	Gave low interest loans to farmers to help them pay their debts such as mortgages. Twenty per cent of farmers benefited from the scheme.
Federal Emergency Relief Administration (FERA)	Provided $500 million for emergency relief through grants to state and local agencies. It was a temporary measure because Roosevelt did not want his opponents to think the government was just handing money out to the unemployed.
National Recovery Administration (NRA)	Set fair prices, wages and working conditions such as maximum hours and **minimum wages**. To encourage business leaders to comply with the codes, the NRA launched a publicity campaign. It adopted as its symbol a blue eagle poster and asked people only to buy goods from businesses displaying the poster. The Act which established the NRA was removed by the Supreme Court in 1935 (see pages 18–19).
Public Works Administration (PWA)	Spent $3,300 million on huge-scale public works.
Reconstruction Finance Corporation (RFC)	Roosevelt pumped $15 billion into Hoover's agency (see page 11). Banks and businesses were able to use some of the money to restart investment.
Tennessee Valley Authority (TVA)	Aimed at regenerating the Tennessee Valley region which was one of the most depressed regions of the USA, with more than half the population of 2.5 million receiving emergency relief and annual flood damage of $1.75 million. The TVA was responsible for creating a system of dams to generate cheap electricity and control flooding in order to attract industry to the area. It also had the power to build recreation areas, as well as to provide health and welfare facilities. Eventually the activities of the TVA covered seven states, an area of 104,000 square kilometres with a population of 7 million people. However, there was some opposition to the TVA from: • farmers whose land was flooded • some big business owners who felt that the USA was moving towards becoming a socialist state.

The key activities and organisations of the Hundred Days

Source B A photograph taken in 1933 showing workers in the Civilian Conservation Corps (CCC)

Source C A cartoon published in a 1933 newspaper: 'The Spirit of the New Deal'

Source D From one of Roosevelt's fireside chats, June 1933. Here he is talking about employers' fair wages

If all employers in each competitive group agree to pay their workers the same reasonable wages – and require the same hours – reasonable hours – then higher wages will hurt no employer. Such action is better for the employer than unemployment and low wages, because it makes more buyers for his product. That is the simple idea which is at the very heart of the Industrial Recovery Act.

TASKS

4 Using the information in the table on page 14 divide the alphabet agencies into three groups: 1 Relief, 2 Recovery, 3 Reform. What do you notice about your decisions?

5 Study Source B. What does it show you about the role of the CCC?

6 Use Sources C and D and your own knowledge to explain how Roosevelt helped industry.

7 Describe the New Deal measures put in place to help agriculture. (For guidance on how to answer this type of question, see pages 41–42.)

The second New Deal

By the end of 1934 there were still 10 million Americans out of work. In January 1935, in his yearly message to Congress, Roosevelt introduced his second New Deal, a broad programme of reform to help farmers, workers, the poor and the unemployed.

The Works Progress Administration (WPA)

This was headed by Harry Hopkins (who had previously been in charge of FERA, see page 14) who was quick to put the programme into action. The mainstay of the programme was funding and building projects, including hospitals, schools, airports, harbours, etc., thus creating employment. It:

- organised a $4.8 billion relief programme
- put unemployed teachers back to work
- created community service schemes to employ artists, writers and actors.

Roosevelt described the work of the WPA as 'priming the pump' – in other words, the government was acting by re-starting the machinery of the economy.

Source E A cartoon from 1935: 'Roosevelt the friend of the poor'

The National Labour Relations Act (The Wagner Act)

Roosevelt was keen to protect the rights of workers. The Wagner Act upheld the right of workers to organise and enter into **collective bargaining**. The number of **labour union** members increased from 3 million in 1933 to 9 million six years later. The Act also set up the National Relations Board, which was given the power to act against employers who used unfair practices, such as sacking workers who had joined the union.

Fair Labour Standards Act

By this Act:

- minimum wages and maximum hours were established for all employees of business engaged in interstate commerce
- 300,000 workers secured higher wages as a result and more than 1 million had a shorter working week
- child labour was not permitted except on farms.

Social Security Act

This was perhaps the most important reform of the second New Deal because by passing this Act the government at last accepted full responsibility for meeting the basic needs of its citizens. The Act established:

- pension benefits for the elderly, the orphaned and those injured in industrial accidents
- unemployment benefits, which would be funded by a tax on the payrolls of employers.

TASK

8 What is the message of Source E?

▶ How successful was the New Deal?

The New Deal achieved a number of successes but also had failures and shortcomings.

Role of government and the president

1 The New Deal restored the faith of people in government after the *laissez-faire* approach of Hoover.
2 It preserved democracy and ensured there was no mass support of right-wing politicians.
3 It greatly extended the role of central government and the president.
4 Roosevelt gave too much power to the federal government and the presidency. The federal government was becoming directly involved in areas which had traditionally been managed by state governments.

Economy

1 The New Deal stabilised the US banking system and cut the number of business failures.
2 It provided only short-term solutions and did not solve the underlying economic problems.
3 It greatly improved the infrastructure of the USA by providing roads, schools and power stations.
4 The US economy took longer to recover than that of most European countries. When, in 1937, Roosevelt reduced the New Deal budget, the country went back into depression.

Unemployment and industrial workers

1 The Alphabet Agencies provided only short-term jobs. Once these ended, people were back on the dole. Even at its best in 1937, there were still over 14 million out of work. It was the Second World War that brought an end to unemployment.
2 The Alphabet Agencies provided work for millions: unemployment fell from a peak of 24.9 million in 1933 to 14.3 million four years later.
3 The NRA and the second New Deal greatly strengthened the position of **labour unions** and made corporations negotiate with them.
4 Unions were still treated with great suspicion by employers. Indeed, many strikes were broken up with brutal violence in the 1930s.

Social welfare

1 The Social Security Act provided the USA with a semi-welfare state which included pensions for the elderly and widows and state help for the sick and disabled.
2 Some argued that social welfare measures put too much pressure on taxpayers and encouraged people to 'sponge' off the state.

Black Americans

1 Many New Deal agencies discriminated against black people. They either got no work, or received worse treatment or lower wages than their white colleagues.
2 Around 200,000 black Americans gained benefits from the CCC (see page 14) and other New Deal Agencies. Many benefited from slum clearance programmes and housing projects.
3 Roosevelt did little to end segregation and discrimination in the Deep South.

Women

1 Some state governments tried to avoid social security payments to women by introducing special qualifications.
2 Some women achieved prominent positions in the New Deal. Eleanor Roosevelt became an important campaigner for social reform. Frances Perkins (see Source A, page 13) was the first woman to be appointed to a cabinet post as Secretary of Labour.
3 Some of the National Industry Recovery Act codes of 1933 actually required women to be paid less than men.
4 Only 8,000 women were employed by the CCC out of the 2.75 million people involved in it.

TASKS

9 Organise the statements on this page into successes and failures of the New Deal.

10 How successful was the New Deal? (For guidance on how to answer this type of question, see page 96.)

Why was there opposition to the New Deal?

The New Deal aroused opposition from a number of individuals and groups as well as the Supreme Court.

▶ Individuals

The New Deal was criticised by individuals who believed that Roosevelt was not doing enough. They had their own ideas about what he should be doing.

● Huey Long had been Governor of the State of Louisiana. He claimed that Roosevelt failed to share out the nation's wealth fairly and announced his own plans to do this under the slogan 'Share Our Wealth'. Long attracted much support but was killed by a doctor whose career he had ruined.

● Father Charles Coughlin criticised the New Deal for not doing enough and labelled Roosevelt as 'anti-God' because he was not really helping the needy. Father Coughlin's main influence came from his weekly broadcasts which attracted over 40 million listeners.

● Dr Frances Townsend gained much support from the elderly who, in 1934, had benefited little from the New Deal. He set up an organisation called 'Old Age Revolving Pension Plan', also known as the Townsend clubs, which had attracted 5 million members by 1935.

▶ Opposition from politicians

Roosevelt also faced opposition from a variety of political groups.

● The **Republicans** were strong opponents of the New Deal. Not only were they traditional opponents of the **Democrats**, they were also the party which represented the interests of America's rich families and large business corporations. These people believed that Roosevelt was doing too much to help people and was changing the accepted role of government in the USA.

● The American Liberty League was set up in 1934 to preserve individual freedom and was backed by wealthy businessmen; two of these, Alfred Smith and John Davis, rather surprisingly had previously stood as Democrat presidential candidates. The League believed that the New Deal threatened the Constitution of the USA and the freedom of the individual.

● Even some members of Roosevelt's own party, the Democrats, opposed the New Deal. They were known as Conservative Democrats, many of whom came from the South and represented farming areas. They were especially against the Wagner Act (see page 16) which had given greater powers to the trade unions.

Source A From a 1936 manifesto for the Republican Party

America is in peril. For three long years the New Deal administration has dishonoured the American traditions and betrayed the pledges upon which the Democratic Party sought and received public support. The rights and liberties of American citizens have been violated. It has created a vast multitude of new offices, filled them with its favourites, set up a centralised bureaucracy and sent out swarms of inspectors to harass our people.

▶ The Supreme Court

One reason that the Supreme Court opposed some of Roosevelt's measures was that the court was dominated by Republican judges. This was because from 1861 to 1933 there were only sixteen years of Democrat presidents and few opportunities to nominate Democrat judges.

Out of the sixteen cases concerning the Alphabet Agencies which were tried by the Supreme Court in 1935 and 1936, the judges declared that, in eleven cases, Roosevelt had acted unconstitutionally. In reality, he was using central or federal powers which the Constitution had not given him. The two cases below show the opposition he faced.

The 'Sick Chickens' case, 1935

This involved four brothers, the Schechters, who ran a poultry business. In 1933 they signed the rules of the National Recovery Administration (NRA) which had been set up by the National Industrial Recovery Act (NIRA). These rules governed fair prices, wages and competition. In 1935, the NRA took them to court for selling a batch of diseased chickens unfit for human consumption. The Schechters appealed to the Supreme Court which declared the NIRA illegal because its activities were unconstitutional. It gave the federal government powers that it should not have to interfere in state affairs, in this case the state of New York. As a result, 750 of the NRA codes of practice were immediately scrapped.

The *US v. Butler* case, 1936

In this case the Supreme Court declared the Agricultural Adjustment Act illegal. The judges decided that giving help to farmers was a matter for each state government, not the federal government. As a result all help to farmers ceased.

Source B A cartoon of 1936 showing Roosevelt lassoing a Supreme Court judge

THE LINE OF LEAST RESISTANCE

Roosevelt's attempts at reform

After his massive victory in the 1936 presidential election, Roosevelt decided that public opinion was behind his New Deal. Therefore, in February 1937, he threatened to retire those judges in the Supreme Court who were over 70, and replace them with younger ones who supported his policies.

These attempts failed for two reasons. First, many saw this as unconstitutional. They saw the President as trying to destroy the position of the Supreme Court by packing it with his own supporters. Secondly, Roosevelt failed to consult senior members of his own party and many Conservative Democrats opposed his reform.

Nevertheless, in March/April 1937 the Supreme Court reversed the 'Sick Chickens' decision and accepted his Social Security Act which brought in old-age pensions and unemployment insurance (see page 16). On the other hand, the whole episode had damaged Roosevelt's reputation and lost him the support of some members of his own party.

TASKS

1 Describe the opposition of individuals to the New Deal. (For guidance on how to answer this type of question, see pages 41–42.)

2 Explain why many Republicans opposed the New Deal. You may wish to use Source A for information.

3 Study Source B. What does it suggest about Roosevelt's relationship with the Supreme Court?

4 Put together your own mind map showing the reasons why there was opposition to the New Deal. Place your reasons in rank order clockwise, beginning with the most important reason at 12 o'clock.

5 How successful was opposition to the New Deal? (For guidance on how to answer this type of question, see page 96.)

What impact did the Second World War have on the US economy?

On 7 December 1941, the Japanese launched an attack on the American fleet at Pearl Harbor, resulting in the deaths of 2,400 Americans. Within four days the USA was at war with Japan and Germany. The Second World War brought about important economic changes.

Changes in the role of government

The New Deal had greatly changed the role of the federal government in the economy (see pages 13–17). This was further extended during the war. For example, in 1942, Roosevelt set up the War Production Board under the **industrialist** William Knusden, to organise and provide for the needs of war and especially the needs of the armed forces. To help promote support for the war, the government set up schemes such as the Office for Civilian Defence, which asked the American people to give 'an hour a day for the USA'. By 1945, the government employed almost 4 million civilian workers, almost double the number of 1941.

Big business and the war effort

Roosevelt was determined to make use of leading US businessmen to provide for the needs of war. The War Production Board was run by a leading industrialist whilst another important industrialist, Henry J Kaiser, had been heavily involved in the Tennessee Valley Authority (see page 14). Roosevelt called in other industrialists to ask their advice on meeting the demands of wartime production and setting targets, allowing them to decide which companies would produce particular goods. For example, **General Motors** produced heavy machine guns and thousands of other war products. Indeed, the vast majority of contracts went to larger firms. In return, the firms made a lot of money.

Source A From the diary of Henry Stimson, the US Secretary of War, 1941

If we are going to war in a capitalist country we've go to let business make money out of the process or business doesn't work.

Wartime production

The USA became the arsenal of the **Allied powers**. Roosevelt believed that to win a modern war you had to have more of everything than your opponents. Traditional industries such as coal, iron, steel and oil greatly expanded due to government contracts.

In 1939, the USA had a very small air force of just 300 planes. In 1944, the USA built 96,000 aircraft in one year alone, more than Germany and Japan combined. Between 1941 and 1945 American factories produced 250,000 aircraft, 90,000 tanks, 350 naval destroyers, 200 submarines and 5,600 merchant ships. Indeed, by 1944 the USA was producing almost half the weapons in the world.

The workforce

As a result of **conscription** (compulsory military service) about 16 million American men and women served in the US armed forces. This meant that many more workers were needed on the home front. This, in turn, put an end to the serious problem of unemployment caused by the Depression. In 1939, unemployment stood at 9.5 million. By 1944, it had fallen to 670,000. Fourteen million people worked in the factories. For example, General Motors took on an extra 750,000 workers during the war. Nearly 4 million workers, many of these black Americans, **migrated** from the rural South to the industrial North.

Probably the greatest change was in the employment of women. Although there were already 12 million working women in the USA, a further 7 million joined the workforce, taking on jobs from which they had previously been excluded. For example, one in three aircraft workers were women, and half of those working in electronics and **munitions** were also women.

General benefits

Of all the countries involved in the Second World War, the USA was the only one that became stronger economically.

- More than half a million new businesses were set up.
- American farmers enjoyed much better times as the US exported food to help its allies.

The US government raised the money to finance the war by raising taxes and by selling **bonds** to the public. Those buying the bonds were guaranteed their money back after a set period plus a guaranteed rate of interest. By the end of the war, Americans had bought bonds totalling $129 billion.

Source B A US government poster advertising war bonds, December 1941. The slogan reads, 'Buy Defense bonds and stamps now'

TASKS

1 Study Source A. What incentive to business is suggested by Stimson?

2 Study Source B. What is the main message of the poster?

3 Explain why unemployment fell during the war years.

4 Was the Second World War a turning point in the recovery of the US economy? (For guidance on how to answer this type of question, see pages 75–76.)

5 What was the most important factor in bringing about change to the US economy in the years 1930–45? In your answer you may wish to discuss the following:

- the Depression
- the New Deal
- the Second World War

and any other relevant factors.

(For guidance on how to answer this type of question, see pages 108–110.)

Examination practice

Here is an opportunity for you to practise an example of Question 1 from Section A.

Question 1: This question is about Changing Life in the USA, 1930–2000

(a) Outline the main features of the Watergate Scandal. (5 marks)

- You will need to describe at least three key features.
- Be specific, avoid generalised comments.
- For further guidance, see pages 41–42.

(b) Look at these two sources about life for women in the USA and answer the question that follows.

Source A From a GCSE history website

In the 1950s, the majority of Americans believed that a woman's place was in the home. The growth of the consumer society allowed women to use labour saving devices and convenience foods at home.

Source B From a school history textbook

By the mid 1960s there were 1.5 million women at university in the USA. This suggests that many women were becoming increasingly bored and frustrated with life in comfortable suburbia.

Explain why life changed for many women in the USA by the 1960s. (7 marks)

[In your answer you should use the information in the sources and your own knowledge to show the extent of change and the reasons for this.]

- You must make direct reference to the content of each source, describing and expanding upon the key points, showing the change that took place.
- Provide context by bringing in your own knowledge of this topic area, highlighting the changes and, if necessary, the reasons for those changes.
- For further guidance, see pages 60–62.

(c) How successful was the New Deal in helping American people during the Depression of the early 1930s? (8 marks)

- You must evaluate the importance or significance of the named individual, event or issue.
- Make reference to the key word in the question – importance, significance or turning point.
- The question requires you to make a judgement and to support it with specific factual detail.
- For further guidance, see page 96.

2 What were the main political and economic developments in the USA after 1945?

Source A A photograph of a US family in the 1950s

TASK

Study Source A. What does it suggest about life in the USA in the 1950s?

In the years 1945–2000 the USA experienced profound political and economic developments. Many middle class Americans abandoned the centre of cities for the suburbs and there was growing affluence for some. Politically, the 'Red Scare' and McCarthyism of the 1950s gave way to the New Frontier of Kennedy and the Great Society of Johnson in the 1960s. The Watergate Scandal dominated the 1970s but was followed by important domestic changes by Presidents Reagan, Bush Snr and Clinton.

This chapter addresses the following issues:

- How did life change in the 1950s?
- What was the Red Scare?
- What was McCarthyism and why did it fade away?
- What changes were introduced by the New Frontier and the Great Society?
- The key measures of the New Frontier and Great Society
- What were the key features of the Watergate Scandal?
- Effects of the scandal
- What domestic changes were brought in by Presidents Reagan, Bush Snr and Clinton?

Examination guidance
Throughout this chapter you will be given the opportunity to practise different exam-style questions. You will be given guidance on how to approach tasks like those in question (a) in Unit 3. This is the describe/outline question which requires you to provide specific knowledge of an historical event. It is worth 5 marks.

How did life change in the 1950s?

After President Roosevelt's unexpected death on 12 April 1945, Vice President Harry Truman was sworn in as the new president. He introduced a programme of economic development and social welfare which became known as the Fair Deal. In his 1949 **State of the Union Address** to Congress, Truman stated that 'Every segment of our population, and every individual, has a right to expect from his government a fair deal.' This policy was continued by his successor, Eisenhower, and led to the prosperity of the 1950s.

▶ Suburbia

The idea of suburbia was a new development in the 1950s. Many middle-class families abandoned the centre of cities and moved to new homes in the suburbs. The suburbanisation of the United States was a central part of the campaign to create the ideal American family, and the federal government played a direct role in the mass migration from the cities. This movement was due to several factors:

● Suburbia embodied the 'American Dream' for many young couples in post-war America as a place where they could own their own home and raise their children away from the horrors of city life.

● Houses were reasonably priced and made affordable to newly married middle-class couples through low-interest mortgages.

● Most families had at least one car which meant that people no longer had to live close to their place of work.

● The economic growth and affluence of the post-war years made these new houses and consumer goods affordable to an increasing number of Americans.

● Between 1945 and 1960, a '**baby boom**' increased the population by about 40 million and increased the demand for new homes. The number of home owners increased from 23,600,000 in 1950 to 32,800,00 in 1960.

By 1960 over 20 per cent of American families lived in homes that had been built in the 1950s. These homes included all the 'mod-cons' such as televisions, washing machines and fridges. Owning a car or the latest hi-fi record player, or perhaps installing a swimming pool, became important status symbols in suburbia. The invention of the transistor, which replaced large and costly valves in such things as radios and televisions, revolutionised the manufacture of electric circuits. By 1960, 90 per cent of homes had television sets, which changed the pattern of daily life.

However, many women who were unable to go out to work felt isolated and bored in their new suburban homes and looked for companionship. They organised **Tupperware parties** where they met over coffee to buy kitchen products. One writer of the time, Lewis Mumford, was very critical of suburbia.

Source A A table comparing the percentage of American families owning consumer goods in 1950 and 1956

	Cars	Televisions	Refrigerators	Washing machines
1950	60.0	26.4	86.4	71.9
1956	73.0	81.0	96.0	86.8

Affluence

The statistics (see Source A on page 24) seem to suggest an affluent society getting richer. There were several reasons for this:

- Americans spent $100 billion they had saved during the Second World War. Much of this money went on consumer goods, especially televisions and cars.
- Hire purchase, known as consumer credit, increased by 800 per cent between 1945 and 1957.
- The improved efficiency of the workforce meant that consumer goods could be produced more cheaply, which kept down prices.
- The growth in population (see page 24) also provided a greater demand for goods.
- Finally, the Korean War (1950–53) and the ongoing **Cold War** meant that American industries were kept busy turning out new weapons which led to big orders for industries such as steel, coal and electronics.

In 1960, the standard of living of the average American was three times that of the average Briton. They were encouraged to spend and shopping became a popular recreational activity. The average wages of factory workers went up from $55 per week in 1950 to $80 in 1959.

Movies and magazines carried the news of American success to millions of envious people around the world. Vast supermarkets, new freeways, large cars with fins and chrome, and television games were all, it was claimed, symbols of a flourishing economy and a free society.

Source B From William E. Leuchtenberg, *A Troubled Feast, American Society Since 1945*, published in 1973

When the Paris Editor of the 'U.S. News and World Report' came home to the United States in 1960 after twelve years abroad, he was astonished at the changes. He had been living in France where only one family in ten had a bath tub with hot running water and was coming home to a country where, in some sections of California, at least one family in ten owned a swimming pool. With larger incomes than ever before there were, for consumers, shopping precincts with piped music, and supermarkets with row on row of brilliantly coloured cartoons.

The 'other America'

However, not every American shared in this new-found affluence.

- Many Americans, including black Americans, remained part of an underclass that was unable to share in the prosperity. In 1959, 29 per cent of the population lived below the poverty line.
- People's income was also affected by the area in which they lived. People in the southern states, in particular, remained well behind those of the north or the west coast.
- There was no national health service and the cost of medical care rose very rapidly. The USA lagged behind many European countries in providing good pensions and welfare services.

Source C Part of a speech by Adlai Stevenson, a Democrat Senator, in 1952

How can we talk about prosperity to the sick who cannot afford proper medical care? How can we talk about prosperity to the hundreds of thousands who can find no decent place to live at prices they can afford? And how can we talk about prosperity to a sharecropper living on worn-out land, or to city dwellers packed six to a room in a unit tenement with a garbage-strewn alley for their children's playground? To these people, national prosperity is a mockery – to the 11 million families in this nation with incomes of less than $2,000 a year.

TASKS

1 Describe the main features of life in suburbia in the 1950s. (For guidance on how to answer this type of question, see pages 41–42.)

2 Explain why people moved to the suburbs in the 1950s.

3 Look at Sources B and C which are about life in the USA during the 1950s and 1960s. Explain why US society became more affluent during the 1950s and 1960s. (For guidance on how to answer this type of question, see pages 60–62.)

What was the Red Scare?

In the later 1940s and early 1950s there was a growing fear of communism in the USA which was known as the **Red Scare**. This fear was due to events inside and outside of America.

▶ The impact of the Cold War

Fear of communism developed in the USA in the years after the **Bolshevik Revolution** of 1917 in Russia. Although the USA and the **Soviet Union** were allies during the Second World War, American distrust of communism continued. In the years after 1945 a 'cold war' developed between the USA and the Soviet Union. This led to an increase in fear and hatred of communism by most Americans. It became known as the Red Scare. Communists or those thought to have communist sympathies faced great intolerance and the eventual loss of their political and other rights. 'Better dead than Red' became a popular slogan.

Soviet control of countries in Eastern Europe in the years after the Second World War led to fears of further communist expansion in Europe. However, the success of the Communist Party in China in 1949 indicated the 'danger' of communism was a truly worldwide threat. The invasion of South Korea by communist North Korea, supported by China and the Soviet Union, in 1950, seemed to confirm all these fears. The result was a wave of anti-communist hysteria in the USA.

Source A The front cover of the propaganda comic book *Is This Tomorrow*, published in America in 1947

The Red Scare, 1945–50

The fear of communism was intensified by developments in the USA in the years after 1945.

President Truman disliked communism and he often talked about 'the enemy within' – meaning inside the USA – whilst the Federal Bureau of Investigation (**FBI**) had a strong anti-communist director, J. Edgar Hoover. He was the driving influence behind the Federal Employee Loyalty Programme (FELP) which he used to investigate government employees to see if they were members of the Communist Party.

Source B J Edgar Hoover, speaking in 1947

Communism, in reality, is not a political party. It is a way of life, an evil and malignant way of life. It reveals a condition akin to a disease that spreads like an epidemic and, like an epidemic, a quarantine is necessary to keep it from infecting the nation.

The Hollywood Ten

Later in 1947, the House Un-American Activities Committee (HUAC) began to look into communist infiltration of the film industry. There was a fear that films were being used to put over a communist message. Ten writers and directors had to testify before HUAC and they were asked if they had ever been members of the Communist Party. When they refused to answer, pleading the **Fifth Amendment**, they were found to be in contempt of Congress. The **Hollywood Ten** were sacked and spent a year in prison.

The Hiss and Rosenberg cases

The Hiss and Rosenberg court cases intensified the fear of communism.

In 1948 Whittaker Chambers, an editor on *Time* magazine and a former communist, informed a leading member of HUAC, Richard Nixon, that Alger Hiss, a high ranking member of the US State Department, was a spy. Hiss had worked for a Supreme Court judge, and in 1948 was working for a peace organisation. Hiss was interrogated and discredited by Nixon, but there was little evidence to prove him to be a spy.

Later that year, Nixon and one of his assistants were invited to Chambers' farm. Chambers took Nixon and

his aide to a pumpkin patch where he pulled off the top of a pumpkin and took out a roll of microfilm. The microfilm held government documents, some of which had been copied on Hiss' typewriter. The documents became known as the 'Pumpkin Papers'. In 1950, Hiss was tried for perjury and sentenced to five years in jail. Nixon became known as a relentless pursuer of communists.

The Soviet Union exploded its first atomic bomb in August 1949, several years sooner than the USA had expected. Some in America believed this could only have been achieved so quickly due to spying. That same month, Julius Rosenberg and his wife Ethel were arrested on suspicion of spying and later tried on the charge of conspiring to commit espionage. The couple were former members of the Communist Party but had no links to it by 1949. However, the government claimed that they were intending to give atomic secrets to the Soviet Union. Both were found guilty and sentenced to death. They were executed on the same day in June 1953.

In September 1950, at the height of the Hiss case and just after the Rosenberg case and the worry over Korea, Congress passed the McCarran Internal Security Act which meant that:

- The Communist Party had to register with the justice department to ensure that the party and its members could be carefully monitored.
- In the event of war, suspected communists could be held in detention camps.
- A Subversive Activities Control Board was set up to watch communist activities in the USA.
- Communists were not allowed to work in armament factories.

TASKS

1 What is the message of Source A?

2 Explain why the Red Scare developed in the USA after 1945. You may wish to use Source B for information.

3 Describe the events that led to the arrest of Hiss and Rosenberg. (For guidance on how to answer this style of question, see pages 41–42.)

4 Construct a mind map showing the main reasons for the growing fear of communism in the USA in the years after 1945.

What was McCarthyism and why did it fade away?

At the height of the fears in 1950, there appeared a **senator** who in a very short time created hysteria about communism. This was Senator Joseph McCarthy of Wisconsin. He became the symbol of the 'red-hating crusader' and gave his name to the era – McCarthyism.

On 9 February 1950, McCarthy addressed a **Republican** meeting in West Virginia and stated that he had the names of 205 communists who were working in the **State Department**, which dealt with foreign affairs.

Source A From a speech by Senator Joe McCarthy, January 1950

While I cannot take the time to name all the men in the State Department who have been named as members of the Communist Party and members of a spy ring, I have here in my hand a list of 205 that are known to the Secretary of State as being members of the Communist Party and are still working and shaping the policy of the State Department.

McCarthy was made Chairman of the Government Committee on Operations of the Senate and this allowed him to investigate state bodies and also interview hundreds of individuals about their political beliefs. His aim was to root out communists from the government, and his hearings and public statements destroyed the lives of many people.

Little evidence was produced by McCarthy – it was enough to be accused by him. Nevertheless, he won massive support across the USA and it is clear that in 1952, his activities contributed to the Republicans' presidential victory. McCarthy continued his work of hunting out communists and, in late 1952, his researchers investigated libraries to see whether they contained any anti-American books which might have been written by communists. As a result of the searches, many of these books were taken out of circulation.

▶ McCarthy's fall

McCarthyism faded away in the mid-1950s for several reasons.

- McCarthy sealed his own fate when he began to cast doubts about the security of the army. His investigations were televised from April to June 1954 and, in these, the American public saw for the first time the true nature of the man. He never produced any hard evidence and relied on rumour and bluff. Furthermore, McCarthy was very aggressive in his questioning of witnesses – some felt he bullied in his cross-examinations. The army attorney, Joseph Welch, approached the hearing in a calm and measured manner, in contrast to McCarthy. The claims against the army were seen to be unfounded and McCarthy himself now faced challenges.
- There had already been a television programme in March 1954 which condemned McCarthy. The acclaimed journalist, Ed Murrow (see Source B), produced a programme based almost entirely on McCarthy's words and this showed clearly the shabby nature of all the baseless claims.
- Other journalists began to attack McCarthy and, at last, those who had feared him now had the confidence to express their views openly.
- In December 1954, McCarthy was publicly reprimanded by the **Senate** for contempt of a Senate elections sub-committee, abuse of certain senators and insults to the Senate during the very hearings which condemned him. McCarthy then lost the chairmanship of the Committee on Operations of the Senate and this signalled the end of his power. For many, his death in 1957 was not a time for mourning.

Source B Ed Murrow, a leading American journalist, 9 March 1954, attacking McCarthyism

The line between investigating and persecuting is a very fine one and … [McCarthy] has stepped over it repeatedly. This is no time for those who oppose him to keep quiet.

▶ The effects of McCarthyism

McCarthy's brief time as 'Communist-finder General' had divided the USA and his influence lived on after him.

● The words 'red', 'pinko', 'commie' and 'lefty' became synonymous with someone who was politically unsound, unpatriotic and therefore a threat to the USA.
● McCarthy had created a climate of fear. There was much spying on neighbours, and government films encouraged people to expose anyone who were thought to have communist sympathies.
● Anyone who sought to change the USA – for example, bringing in **civil rights** for black Americans – was seen as a communist.
● The hatred of communism never really died away.

TASKS

1 Look at Sources A and B which are about McCarthyism. Explain why attitudes towards the threat of communism had changed by the mid–1950s. (For guidance on how to answer this type of question, see pages 60–62.)

2 Draw a McCarthy-style poster warning Americans about the dangers of the spread of communism in the USA.

3 What is the message of Source C?

4 Explain why McCarthy lost support in the mid-1950s.

5 'REDS UNDER THE BEDS': this was a famous anti-communist headline of the 1950s in the USA. Working with a partner, put together three or four more of these anti-communist headlines.

6 Describe the effects of McCarthyism on the people of the USA. (For guidance on how to answer this type of question, see pages 41–42.)

Source C A cartoon about McCarthy by Edwin Marcus, 1954

What changes were introduced by the New Frontier and the Great Society?

In the 1960s Presidents Kennedy and Johnson introduced a series of important changes to US society known as the **New Frontier** and the **Great Society**.

▶ Kennedy and the New Frontier

Kennedy won the presidential election campaign of 1960 and was president until his assassination in 1963. In his acceptance speech as president he mentioned the 'New Frontier'.

At first it was simply a slogan to try to unite and inspire the American people and get them behind him. However, it soon became a programme of reform and change in which Kennedy hoped to make the US a fairer society by giving equal rights to all black people, and by helping them to better themselves. He called it the New Frontier to make people feel excited and try to reduce opposition to it. Above all else he wanted to make the USA a fairer and better place and he asked Americans to join him in being 'New Frontiersmen'.

Opposition to the New Frontier

Kennedy faced opposition in Congress to his ideas.

- His own position as president was not strong as he had won only by a narrow margin in the 1960 presidential campaign.
- Many older members of Congress felt he was too young and inexperienced and distrusted his '**Brains Trust**' appointments.
- Some were suspicious of the radical nature of his 'New Frontier' and the pace of change and saw it as a **socialist** programme.
- He was the first Catholic president. This again created suspicion from the more traditional Protestant politicians.

- The greatest opposition came from Southern Congressmen, even Democrats – members of his own party – who disliked his commitment to civil rights. They felt that equal rights for black Americans would cost them the votes of whites in the South.

Despite his charm and charisma, Kennedy found it difficult to deal with Congress and many of his bills were rejected. However, he was successful in increasing social security, raising the minimum wage and setting up training schemes for the unemployed. His early death meant he was unable to complete his programme of reform.

▶ The Great Society

Lyndon Johnson was president from 1963 to 1968. His achievements have often been underestimated and overlooked due to the reputation of Kennedy and the US involvement in the war in Vietnam.

Johnson decided to continue the work of Kennedy and carry it further. In his first speech as president he talked of a 'Great Society' which would declare war on poverty. To do this he planned to improve the health of the poor and the old by providing them with a better diet and living conditions. He called for 'an immediate end to racial injustice', especially racial discrimination in employment and education. Johnson tackled areas that Kennedy had not been able to improve such as medical care for the poor.

Johnson was an experienced politician who knew how to get things done and how to make deals with

Congress. He was far more successful than nearly any other president in getting measures passed through Congress. Also, because he was a Southerner, he knew how to deal with the Southern Democrats and overcome their opposition – especially to civil rights. Some believe his six-foot-five-inch frame helped him to dominate others.

Opposition to the Great Society

Just like Kennedy with his policies, Johnson faced powerful opposition to his Great Society measures. This opposition, however, was distorted due to attitudes to US involvement in the war in Vietnam.

Source A A cartoon showing President Johnson and the Great Society, from the British magazine *Punch*, 1967. It shows him breaking up the 'Great Society'

The Train Robbery

- Republicans accused him of wasting money on welfare programmes and of undermining 'rugged individualism'. He was accused of overspending on welfare programmes.
- He was accused of doing too little to tackle the problems of the inner cities. In 1967 there was serious rioting in several cities including six days in Watts, the black district of Los Angeles (see page 101).
- The greatest problem for Johnson was the escalation of the US involvement in the war in Vietnam. This was not only costly, meaning spending was diverted from the Great Society to paying for the war, but it led to increasing criticism of Johnson himself (see page 52). His great election victory of 1964 seemed in the distant past as many Americans celebrated his decision not to run for re-election as president in 1968.

TASKS

1 Outline the aims of Kennedy's New Frontier. (For guidance on how to answer this type of question, see pages 41–42.)

2 Explain why there was opposition to the New Frontier.

3 How successful was the New Frontier policy? (For guidance on how to answer this type of question, see page 96.)

4 Describe Johnson's Great Society. (For guidance on how to answer this type of question, see pages 41–42.)

5 What is the message of Source A?

6 Draw a two-column table with the headings 'similarities' and 'differences'. Fill it in to show the similarities and differences between the opposition to the policies of Kennedy and Johnson.

The key measures of the New Frontier and Great Society

	The New Frontier
Civil rights	**1** Kennedy appointed five federal judges, including Thurgood Marshall. Marshall was a black American and was a leading civil rights activist. **2** Kennedy threatened legal action against the state of Louisiana for refusing to fund schools which were not segregated. **3** In October 1962, Kennedy sent 23,000 government troops to ensure that one black student, James Meredith, could study at the University of Mississippi (see page 80). **4** Kennedy introduced a Civil Rights Bill to Congress in February 1963. This aimed to give black people equality in housing and education but was defeated in Congress.
The economy	**1** Kennedy deliberately decided not to balance the budget in order to increase economic growth and reduce unemployment. **2** He introduced a general tax cut. More spending would mean more goods sold. **3** There were also public works that cost $900 million. The federal government began a series of projects, such as new roads and public buildings. **4** Grants were given to high-tech companies to invest in high-tech equipment with which to train workers. **5** There was increased spending on defence and space technology, all of which secured or created jobs. Kennedy also promised that the USA would put a man on the moon by the end of the 1960s.
Social reform	**1** Kennedy planned to increase the minimum wage from $1.00 to $1.25 an hour. **2** Kennedy planned to start Medicare, a cheap system of state health insurance. **3** The Manpower and Training Act of 1962 provided retraining for the long-term unemployed. **4** The Area Redevelopment Act of 1961 allowed the federal government to give loans and grants to states with long-term unemployment. **5** The Housing Act of 1961 provided cheap loans for the redevelopment of inner cities. **6** The Social Security Act of 1962 gave greater financial help to the elderly and unemployed. Social security benefits were extended to each child whose father was unemployed.

The Great Society	Who achieved most?
1 The Civil Rights Act of 1964 banned discrimination in public places, in federally assisted programmes and in employment. 2 The Civil Rights Act set up the Equal Opportunity Commission to implement the law. 3 The Voting Rights Act of 1965 appointed agents to ensure that voting procedures were carried out properly (see page 100). 4 In 1967, the Supreme Court declared all laws banning mixed-race marriages were to be removed.	
1 Johnson cut taxes to give consumers more money to spend and, in turn, to help businesses grow and create more jobs. 2 Johnson improved railways and highways. 3 The Appalachian Recovery Programme provided federal funds for the development of the Appalachians, a mountainous area in the eastern states. 4 Manufacturers and shops had to label goods fairly and clearly. Consumers had the right to return faulty goods and exchange them.	
1 The Medical Care Act of 1965 provided Medicare (for the old) and Medicaid (for the poor). This was an attempt to try to ensure that all Americans had equal access to health care. 2 The Elementary and Secondary Education Act, also of 1965, provided the first major federal support for state education ever. Federal money was provided to try to ensure that standards of education in all states were equal. 3 The Model Cities Act of 1966 continued Kennedy's policy of urban renewal. It was in the centres of the big cities that living conditions were at their worst and where crime was highest. The act provided federal funds for slum clearance and the provision of better services. 4 The minimum wage was increased from $1.25 to $1.40 an hour. 5 $1.5 billion was spent on the Head Start Programme so that teachers could provide additional education for very young children from poor backgrounds. 6 The Office of Economic Opportunity set up schemes to help poor people in inner cities. It funded new education projects and community projects and provided loans for local schemes. These schemes were the basis of Johnson's Programme for Poverty.	

TASKS

1 You will have noticed that there are no entries in the last column of the table. Make a copy of the table with the key headings and measures (no need to include the details of the measures themselves). Decide which president achieved the most in each area of reform. Give a brief explanation for each choice.

2 How successful was the Great Society in helping American people during the 1960s? (For guidance on how to answer this type of question, see page 96.)

What were the key features of the Watergate scandal?

Richard Nixon was elected to Congress in 1950 and made a name for himself in the McCarthy anti-communist witch-hunts. He was narrowly defeated by Kennedy in the 1960 presidential election campaign but was successful in 1968 and again in 1972. However, on 8 August 1974, Nixon was forced to resign as president because of the Watergate scandal which began in 1972.

▶ Events of the scandal

CREEP

In 1968, Richard Nixon, the Republican candidate, was elected president. In 1972 he would have to seek re-election. Concerned that he might not be re-elected, he set up CREEP – Committee to Re-Elect the President. It was encouraged to use whatever methods necessary to ensure his re-election with $350,000 set aside for 'dirty tricks'.

The break-in

On 17 June 1972, five members of CREEP were arrested for breaking into the Watergate offices of the Democrat Party. It soon became obvious that they were not ordinary burglars but were there to plant bugging devices.

The *Washington Post* reporters

Two reporters from the *Washington Post*, Carl Bernstein and Bob Woodward, discovered that all five burglars were employed by CREEP and that the CREEP fund was controlled by the White House. Nixon strongly denied any involvement by himself and his advisers. Nixon won a landslide victory in the 1972 presidential election.

Source A A cartoon in the *Washington Post*, 1973

A 1973 Herblock Cartoon, copyright by The Herb Block Foundation

The trial of the burglars

In January 1973, the Watergate burglars went on trial and were all convicted. In March, James McCord, one of those convicted, claimed in court that there had been a White House cover-up. Again Nixon denied all knowledge of the break-in or cover-up. However, he did admit that two of his top advisers, Bob Haldeman and John Ehrlichman, had been involved. They resigned on 30 April 1973.

Source B From the tapes of 21 March 1973, describing attempts at a cover-up

Dean: That's right. Plus there is a real problem in raising money. Mitchell has been working on raising money. He is one of the ones with the most to lose. But there is no denying the fact that the White House, in Ehrlichman and Haldeman, are involved in the early money decisions.

President: How much money do you need?

Dean: I would say these people are going to cost a million dollars over the next two years

President: You could get a million dollars. You could get it in cash. I know where it could be gotten. But the question is who the hell would handle it. Any ideas?

TASKS

1 What is the message of Source A?

2 Outline the events which led Richard Nixon to resign as President. (For guidance on how to answer this type of question, see pages 41–42.)

3 Working in pairs, imagine you are editors of the *Washington Post*. Put together a series of headlines to cover the key events of the Watergate scandal.

4 You have just watched Nixon's resignation. Put together a mobile phone text message informing a friend of what you have seen. You may use 'text language'. Remember your word limit – with most mobile phones it is 144 characters.

The Senate Committee
The investigation of a Senate Committee set up to investigate the scandal was televised between May and November 1973. It became increasingly obvious that White House officials had been involved. One of them, John Dean, claimed there had been a cover-up directed by Nixon.

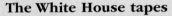

The White House tapes
One White House aide told the Senate Committee that in 1971 Nixon had installed a tape-recording system in the White House and that all the President's conversations had been taped. After at first refusing to hand over the tapes, Nixon handed over seven of the nine tapes on 21 November 1973 but they had been heavily edited. One of them had eighteen minutes missing. Finally, on 30 April 1974, Nixon was made to hand over all the tapes, unedited. They showed that he had been involved in the dirty tricks campaign and had repeatedly lied throughout the investigation. The tapes also shocked the nation because of the foul language used. Any foul language was indicated by the words 'expletive deleted' which occurred at regular intervals.

Nixon resigns
In July 1974, Congress decided to impeach Nixon. This meant that he would be put on trial with the Senate acting as the jury. On 8 August 1974, Nixon resigned, giving his reasons in a televised broadcast, to avoid **impeachment**. His successor, Gerald Ford, issued a decree in September of that year pardoning Nixon for any criminal acts that he had taken part in.

Effects of the scandal

Attitude to politicians
The scandal greatly undermined people's confidence in politics and politicians. In 1976 Americans voted for the presidential election candidate they believed they could trust, Jimmy Carter, who promised never to lie. Even now scandals are generally given the nickname 'gate' after the name of the scandal. One example is the **'Irangate'** scandal of 1987.

Nixon's reputation
It utterly destroyed Nixon's reputation. He was seen as untrustworthy and was given the nickname of 'Tricky Dicky'. For many years afterwards the Watergate scandal overshadowed all his other achievements. Some 31 of Nixon's advisers went to prison for Watergate-related offences.

US Constitution
The Watergate scandal seemed to show how well the legal and political systems worked, as Nixon had been found out and forced to resign. Moreover, the balances of the US Constitution worked well. The Supreme Court had carried out its ultimate function and kept a check on the position of the president.

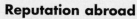

Reputation abroad
The scandal damaged the reputation of the USA abroad and made the USA a laughing stock. The USSR was able to use it as an example of the corruption of the capitalist system. The scandal came, also, at the same time as US troops were being withdrawn from Vietnam, an action that further undermined American self-confidence.

The powers of government
The powers of government were reduced by a series of measures including the:
- Election Campaign Act of 1974 which set limits on election contributions to prevent corruption
- War Powers Act of 1973 which required the president to consult Congress before sending American troops into combat
- Privacy Act of 1974 which allowed citizens to have access to any files that the government may have had on them
- Congressional Budget Act, 1974, which meant that the president could not use government money for his/her own purposes.

TASKS

1 Put together your own concept map showing the effects of the Watergate scandal. Rank order these effects clockwise, beginning with the most important at 12 o'clock.

2 Why was the Watergate scandal a turning point in the politics of the USA in the 1970s? (For guidance on how to answer this type of question, see pages 75–76.)

What domestic changes were brought in by Presidents Reagan, Bush Snr and Clinton?

During the last twenty years of the twentieth century the USA had three different presidents, each with their own domestic policies:

- Ronald Reagan, 1981–89
- George Bush Snr, 1989–93
- Bill Clinton, 1993–2001

▶ Ronald Reagan

President Ronald Reagan

Ronald Reagan, a former film star, won the presidential election campaign of 1980, defeating Jimmy Carter who had served only one term as president from 1977 to 1981. Reagan inherited serious economic problems:

- By 1980 the world recession was biting deeply, bringing factory closures, rising unemployment (to 7.5 per cent) and oil shortages.
- Inflation had risen to nearly 15 per cent and **budget deficits** remained high.

'Reaganomics'

Reagan's economic policies, known as **Reaganomics**, were based on the works of economist Arthur Laffer who argued that cutting taxes for businesses and the wealthier quarter of American citizens would encourage spending and put more money into the economy as a whole. The money would then eventually 'trickle down' or find its way into the middle and lower classes of Americans, making everyone better off. Reagan reasoned that if these tax cuts at the top of society could trickle down and make everyone richer, the government could stop many of its social welfare programmes involving transfers of payments to the poor. In order to carry out these policies Reagan:

- cut welfare programme spending by over $20 billion a year in his first three years, including food stamp programmes and various programmes to assist struggling mothers and children
- slashed taxes. In 1981 the Economic Recovery Tax Act reduced taxes by $33 billion making it the largest tax cut in US history – but to a point where the government was barely collecting any income revenue.

Source A Ronald Reagan speaking in 1981

We who live in free market societies believe that growth, prosperity and ultimately human fulfilment are created from the bottom up, not the government down. Only when the human spirit is allowed to invent, and create, only when individuals are given a personal stake in deciding economic policies … only then can societies remain economically alive, dynamic and free.

TASK

1 What can you learn from Source A about Reaganomics?

The effects of Reaganomics

- Without tax revenues, the government was unable to pay for the services it provided.
- Worse, even though Reagan dramatically reduced tax rates, he actually dramatically increased total government spending, particularly in the areas of defence, which nearly doubled between 1981 and 1987. The government was forced to borrow money each year and the **national debt** rose to its highest ever level at almost $1 trillion. People in all sectors lost their jobs and inflation soared.
- In 1987 Congress, increasingly worried by the rapidly growing federal budget deficit, rejected Reagan's budget for increased defence spending.
- There was a severe stock market crash in 1987, one of the worst stock market crashes since the crash of 1929 (see page 6). This was mainly due to Reagan's economic policies which meant that the USA had the largest trading deficit of any of the leading industrialised nations (when the trade balance was negative and the value of what the USA imported was more than the value of what they exported). At the same time the economy was beginning to slow down as industry moved into **recession**.

President George Bush Snr

The space programme

1986 was a disastrous year for America's space programme.

- In January the space shuttle *Challenger* exploded only seconds after lift-off, killing all seven crew members.
- In April a Titan rocket, carrying secret military equipment, exploded immediately after lift-off.
- In May a Delta rocket failed.
- Moreover, the development of the 'Star Wars' programme (see page 150) had proved very expensive and a further drain on the economy.

These disasters delayed Reagan's plans to develop a permanent orbital space station.

▶ George Bush Snr

In 1988 Vice President George H. Bush Snr succeeded Ronald Reagan as president. He was president for one term until 1992. He had a reputation as a safe pair of hands who was willing to continue with Reagan's domestic policies.

Bush faced the problem of what to do with leftover deficits caused by the Reagan years. At $220 billion in 1990, the deficit had grown to three times its size since 1980. During his election campaign Bush had promised to cut taxes. However, he was forced to go back on his word and increase **indirect taxes** as well as reduce the number of wealthy people exempt from tax. He had to agree to new taxes on the wealthy, a cut in military spending and increased taxes on luxury items. However, the budget deficit continued to rise to $300 billion. The recession developed which reduced government income from taxation even further.

By the end of Bush's presidential term interest and inflation rates were the lowest in years and the unemployment rate reached 7.8 per cent, the highest since 1984. In September 1992, the Census Bureau reported that 14.2 per cent of all Americans lived in poverty.

President Bush Snr signed two significant pieces of domestic legislation during his tenure:

- The Americans with Disabilities Act of 1990, which forbade discrimination based on disability in employment, public accommodations and transportation. This is considered to be the most important anti-discrimination legislation since the Civil Rights Acts of the 1960s.

- The Clean Air Act of 1990 which built on previous legislation of 1963, 1970 and 1977. It focused on three aspects of clean air: reducing urban smog, curbing acid rain, and eliminating industrial emissions of toxic chemicals.

Bush was less successful in other areas:

- He had promised in his election campaign to tackle drug use as his top priority. He gave several billion dollars to the Drug Enforcement Agency which worked on employee drug testing and increased border controls, but this made little impact, especially on those addicted to cocaine and heroin.
- There were race riots in Los Angeles, Atlanta, Birmingham, Seattle and Chicago in 1992 following the arrest and beating of a black man, Rodney King, who had been caught speeding by four white policemen (see page 107). The incident was filmed on a home video camera by a local resident.

TASKS

2 How successful were the economic policies of President Reagan? (For guidance on how to answer this type of question, see page 96.)

3 Should George Bush Snr be regarded as a successful president?

▶ Change under Clinton

In 1992 Bill Clinton defeated George Bush Snr in the presidential election campaign. Clinton was a Democrat, representing the political opposite of his two Republican predecessors, Reagan and Bush Snr, with very different views on the economy and social welfare. The economic downturn was a major reason for his success in the presidential election. By 1992 the gap between the richest and poorest citizens in America had grown even wider, which only served to damage the stability of American society.

There were three major features of Clinton's domestic policies.

1 The move away from Reaganomics

Clinton was determined to reduce the budget deficit left by his predecessors whilst, at the same time, increasing federal government spending and investment in education and welfare.

President Bill Clinton

- He was able to reduce the huge budget deficit left over from the Reagan era. By 1996 he had reduced the deficit to $107 billion and by 1998 the budget was balanced for the first time since 1969.
- He was president during the longest period of sustained economic growth in the history of the USA. The value of the stock market had tripled, the unemployment rate was the lowest for almost 30 years and there was the highest level of home ownership in the history of the USA.
- The North American Free Trade Agreement was signed with Canada and Mexico, setting up a free trade area between the three states and stimulating US export markets.

2 Important welfare reforms

In 1996, Clinton introduced a minimum wage of $4.75 an hour which was increased to $5.15 in May 1997. In 1993 he had failed in his ambitious attempt to introduce a system of **universal health insurance**. The Health Security Bill was attacked by the insurance industry and the American Medical Association and was rejected by Congress.

3 A series of scandals

Clinton was linked to the Whitewater scandal of 1996 when two of his former business associates were convicted of multiple fraud over a housing development in the Whitewater area of Arkansas. Although it dragged on for several years, no conclusive evidence was ever found of illegal dealings by Clinton and his wife Hillary.

However, Kenneth Starr, the man leading the Whitewater enquiry, did find proof that Clinton had been having an affair with Monica Lewinsky, a member of the White House staff. Having repeatedly denied any such affair, Clinton was forced to make a public apology to the American people. He was even threatened with impeachment by the House of Representatives but in 1999 the Senate found him not guilty.

Source B Part of President Clinton's televised speech, 17 August 1998

Indeed, I did have a relationship with Ms. Lewinsky that was not appropriate. In fact, it was wrong. It constituted a critical lapse in judgement and a personal failure on my part for which I am solely and completely responsible.

But I told the grand jury today and I say to you now that at no time did I ask anyone to lie, to hide or destroy evidence or to take any other unlawful action. I know that my public comments and my silence about this matter gave a false impression. I misled people, including even my wife. I deeply regret that.

This has gone on too long, cost too much and hurt too many innocent people. Now, this matter is between me, the two people I love most – my wife and our daughter – and our God. I must put it right, and I am prepared to do whatever it takes to do so.

TASKS

4 How successful was President Clinton in reviving the US economy? (For guidance on how to answer this type of question, see page 96.)

5 Use Source B and your own knowledge to explain why there was a scandal over Clinton's relationship with Monica Lewinsky.

6 Make a copy of the following table and summarise the successes and failures of the domestic policies of the three presidents.

	Successes	Failures
Reagan		
Bush Snr		
Clinton		

Examination guidance

This section provides guidance on how to approach tasks like those in question (a) in Unit 3. It is a describe/outline question which requires you to provide specific knowledge of an historical event. It is worth 5 marks.

Describe Kennedy's New Frontier Policy. **(5 marks)**

Two different sample responses to this question are given below and on page 42.

Tips on how to answer

- The question is asking you to **describe** a key historical event.

- Make sure you only include information which is **directly relevant**.

- Jot down your initial thoughts, **making a brief list** of the points you intend to mention.

- After you have finished your list try to put the points into **chronological order** by numbering them.

- It is a good idea to start your answer **using the words of the question.** For example, 'President Kennedy's New Frontier Policy aimed to tackle …'.

- Try to include **specific factual details** such as dates, events, the names of key people, important policies. The more informed your description the higher the mark you will receive.

- Aim to write a **good-sized paragraph**, covering **at least three key features/points**.

Response by Candidate A

Kennedy's New Frontier Policy was aimed at solving America's problems. Kennedy wanted to make life better for many Americans. He hoped to introduce reforms to improve living conditions and help the poor. He planned health reforms. He wanted to help black Americans by passing a civil rights bill which would improve their position in society. Kennedy wanted to change America. He wanted to make things better for the ordinary American.

Comment on Candidate A's performance

This candidate displays an awareness that Kennedy's New Frontier Policy aimed to change America and reference is made to planned improvements in living conditions and health care. Specific reference is made to a civil rights bill. This detail lifts the answer beyond Level One (a generalised response) and into the Level Two band (some detail and accurate description). However, these points will need to be discussed in greater depth to reach Level Three and will require more informed factual support. This response is therefore worthy of a mark [3] at the top end of Level Two.

Response by Candidate B

[Notes by candidate: • many problems facing America[1]
• unemployment[2] • benefits system[4] • health care[5] • civil rights[3]
• education[6]]

President Kennedy aimed to target the key problem areas of poverty and inequality. He planned a series of reforms which would form his 'New Frontier Policy'. He passed bills which led to an expansion of unemployment benefits, an increase in social security benefits and an increase in the minimum wage. He also planned to reform state health insurance (Medicare). An education bill pumped more money into schools and a civil rights bill was planned to grant equality to black Americans. However, he was assassinated before some of these reforms could be completed.

Comment on Candidate B's performance

In contrast to Candidate A this is a detailed and accurate description of Kennedy's 'New Frontier Policy'. The candidate had given some prior thought to the final answer by jotting down a few bullet points which helped to provide a structure to the answer. There was an attempt to identify the problems facing Kennedy when he became president and there was specific detail on how he proposed tackling health care, education and civil rights. The response covered at least three features of the New Frontier Policy. There was sufficient depth of understanding and supportive factual detail to warrant the awarding of maximum [5] marks, placing the answer at the top of Level Three.

Now you have a go:

Outline President Reagan's domestic policies in the 1980s. **(5 marks)**

3 What were the main social developments in the USA from 1945 to 2000?

Source A Journalist Jack Gould writing in the *New York Times* about an Elvis Presley concert, 1956

These gyrations of Elvis's hips have to concern parents unless we're the kind of parents who approve of kids going around stealing hubcaps, indulging in promiscuity [easy sex] and generally behaving like delinquents. It isn't enough to say that Elvis is kind to his parents, sends money home and is the same unspoilt kid as before all the commotion began. That still isn't a free ticket to behave like a sex maniac in public before millions of impressionable kids.

on the young. The 1950s saw the emergence of the teenager and a new and ever changing **youth culture** followed by the student protests and hippy movement of the 1960s. There were also important developments in the position of women in US society, influenced by the Second World War and the **feminist movement** of the 1960s and 1970s.

This chapter addresses the following issues:

- What were the key developments in popular culture?
- How did youth culture change?
- What were the key features of the student movement?
- How did the role of women in the USA change in the years after 1945?

TASK

Put together a headline for Source A.

There were fundamental changes in US society in the second half of the twentieth century. Although the cinema was still important, it was television and later the internet which had the greatest impact, especially

Examination guidance
Throughout this chapter you will be given the opportunity to practise different exam-style questions. You will be given guidance on how to approach tasks like those in question (b) in Unit 3. This requires you to identify and explain the extent of change and/or continuity in a key issue or development through the comparison of two sources and the use of your own knowledge. It is worth 7 marks.

What were the key developments in popular culture?

Popular culture in the second half of the twentieth century in the USA was greatly influenced by the cinema, the dominance of the motor car, the popularity of television and the emergence of the computer and internet.

▶ The cinema

The cinema was popular, but less so than in the inter-war years of 1918–39 because of the growing influence of television. Average weekly cinema attendances fell from 90 million a week in 1946 to 47 million ten years later.

Drive-ins

The **drive-in cinema**, first opened in the 1930s, became very popular in the 1950s and early 1960s, particularly in rural areas, with some 4000 drive-ins spreading across the United States. Among its advantages was the fact that a family with a baby could take care of their child while watching a movie, while teenagers with access to cars found drive-ins ideal for dates. In the 1950s, the greater privacy afforded to patrons gave drive-ins a reputation as immoral, and they were labelled 'passion pits' in the media.

Multiplexes

Stanley H. Durwood became the father of the **multiplex movie theatre** in 1963 when he opened the first ever mall multiplex, made up of two side-by-side theatres with 700 seats, at Ward Parkway Center in Kansas City.

Anti-heroes

In the period following the Second World War young people wanted new and exciting symbols of rebellion. Hollywood responded to audience demands; the late 1940s and 1950s saw the rise of the **anti-hero**, a main character who has a lack of traditional heroic qualities, such as idealism or courage. Newcomers like James Dean (see pages 48–49), Paul Newman and Marlon Brando replaced more traditional actors like Bette Davis, James Cagney, Tyrone Power, Van Johnson and Robert Taylor. In later decades, this new generation of **method actors** would be followed by Robert DeNiro, Jack Nicholson and Al Pacino. Anti-heroines included Ava Gardner, Kim Novak and Marilyn Monroe – an exciting, vibrant, sexy star.

Blockbusters

The 1970s saw the emergence of the blockbuster film, headed up by *Jaws* (1975), directed by the 27-year-old Steven Spielberg. This became the highest grossing film in history – until *Star Wars* two years later which was directed by George Lucas.

Following this model, Hollywood continued to search in the 1980s for the one large 'event film' that everyone, including international audiences, wanted to see. These films had dazzling special effects technology, sophisticated soundtracks, and costly, highly-paid stars. Spielberg followed *Jaws* with *ET* (1982) and teamed up with Lucas for the *Indiana Jones* films of the 1980s, the first of which, *Raiders of the Lost Ark* (1981), made a household name out of the lead actor, Harrison Ford. The video recorder (VCR) encouraged film hire and home viewing and was a further stimulus to the film industry.

The 1990s

In the 1990s, for the most part, cinema attendance was up – mostly at multiplexes throughout the country. It was the decade of the mega-paid movie stars such as Arnold Schwarzenegger, Tom Cruise, Sylvester Stallone, Mel Gibson, Eddie Murphy, Kevin Costner, Harrison Ford, Robin Williams, Jim Carrey, Demi Moore and Julia Roberts. The VCR was still popular in most households (about three-quarters of them had VCRs in 1991) and rentals and purchase of films on videotape were big business – much larger than sales of movie tickets. By 1997, the first DVDs (digital video discs) had emerged in stores, featuring sharper resolution and better quality pictures. Films such as *Jurassic Park* (1993) and *Star Wars Episode I – The Phantom Menace* (1999) used ever more advanced digital imagery and special effects.

▶ The motor car

The motor car, so important in the inter-war years in opening up the suburbs of towns and cities as well as rural areas, continued to influence the development of US society.

- Car ownership increased from 25 million in 1945 to 60 million by 1960. The number of two-car families doubled in the 1950s.
- The 1956 Interstate Highway Act was the largest public works project in American history. It cost $32 billion and led to the construction of 41,000 miles of new highways.
- The motor car made the US a more uniform nation. The first McDonald's was opened in 1955, the same year as Disneyland in Southern California. Forty per cent of the visitors to Disneyland came from outside California and mainly by car.
- Cars encouraged the growth and popularity of the drive-in movie.
- In 1960, Americans owned 61,671,390 cars, or about one car for every three people. By 1970, this had increased to 89,243,557 cars, or almost one car for every two people.

TASK

1 Study Source A. What does it suggest about US society in the 1950s?

Source A An advertisement from 1957 for the Pontiac motor car

▶ Television

During the 1940s, there were relatively few television sets in American homes. However, the number of televisions increased from 7,000 in 1946 to 50 million by 1960. Between 1959 and 1970, the percentage of households in the US with at least one television went from 88 per cent to 96 per cent. Some called television an invention for stupid people to watch. By the end of the 1950s, however, television was here to stay. The average family watched six hours a day. Subscription television (such as cable and satellite) became popular in the early 1980s, and has been growing in significance since then.

Americans especially liked games shows and funny shows with comedians such as Milton Berle and Lucille Ball. They also liked shows that offered a mix of entertainment, such as those presented by Arthur Godfrey and Ed Sullivan. The 'Western' became one of the most popular styles of programme, with popular series including *The Lone Ranger, Bonanza* and *Gunsmoke*. These gave an idealised image of the American West of the nineteenth century.

People from other countries watching American television in the 1950s might have thought that all Americans were white Christians. It celebrated traditional American values. Popular programmes such as *I Love Lucy* and *The Honeymooners* gave a romanticised view of American middle-class suburban life. In a sense, early television created its own view of American culture.

What was portrayed on television came to be accepted as normal. The ideal family, the ideal schools and neighbourhoods, the world, were all seen in a way which had only a partial basis in reality. People began to accept what was heard and seen on television because they were 'eye witnesses' to events as never before. Programmes such as *You Are There* brought historical events into the living rooms of many Americans. At the same time, television failed to recognise that America was a great mix of races and religions. Few members of racial or religious minorities were represented on television. Those who did appear were usually shown to be working for white people.

Source B A scene from the popular television Western of the 1950s, *The Lone Ranger*

Soap operas

American soap operas became, and still are, very popular. Long-running daytime dramas included *Search for Tomorrow* (1951–86), *Love of Life* (1951–80), *The Doctors* (1963–82), *Dallas* (1978–91), *Dynasty* (1981–89) and *Beverly Hills 90210* (1990–2000).

Chat shows

Daytime chat shows such as *Phil Donahue* (1970–96) and *The Jerry Springer Show* (1991–present) have also pulled in many viewers. By far the most successful of these has been the *Oprah Winfrey Show* (often simply referred to as *Oprah* or just *O*) which is the longest-running daytime television chat show in the United States, having run nationally since September 8, 1986. It has featured book clubs, celebrity interviews and self-improvement segments (see also page 105).

▶ Developments in information technology

Personal computers

The 1990s saw a massive growth in the sale of personal computers. This was due mainly to the competition between two rival organisations, Microsoft and Apple.

- Bill Gates set up his company Microsoft in 1975. Microsoft launched its first retail version of Microsoft Windows on November 20, 1985. Gates and Microsoft came to dominate the development of computer electronics, computer software and personal computers.
- The major rival was Apple Computer, Inc. which was set up in California in 1976. The company's best-known hardware products included the Macintosh computers.

The internet

Another major development of the 1990s was the internet.

- In 1991, the first really user-friendly interface to the internet was developed at the University of Minnesota.
- In the following year, Delphi was the first national commercial online service to offer internet access to its subscribers.
- The release of Windows 98 in June 1998 with the Microsoft browser well integrated into the desktop

enabled Bill Gates to take advantage of the enormous growth of the internet.

Gaming

The development of computer generated games became a very significant pastime for the younger generation.

- The first commercially viable video game was *Computer Space* in 1971. In subsequent decades there was massive growth in computer games as well as significant improvements in technology.
- In the 1980s Nintendo introduced the first modern game console called the NES (Nintendo Entertainment System), followed by others such as the Sega Mega Drive, the Sony PlayStation and, in 2001, the Microsoft Xbox.

Impact on US society

These technological developments transformed US society in the last decade of the twentieth century.

- The internet had a drastic impact on culture and commerce. This included the rise of near instant communication by electronic mail (email), text-based discussion forums, and e-commerce.
- More and more leisure time for the younger generation began to be taken up with social networking on the internet as well as the various game consoles. This led to increasing concern for a generation abandoning an active lifestyle for passive activities, resulting in lack of exercise and obesity issues.

TASKS

2 Study Source B. What image does this give of the American West?

3 Explain why television had so much influence on US society in the 1950s and 1960s.

4 How important were the computer and internet in bringing change to US society in the later twentieth century? (For guidance on how to answer this type of question, see page 96).

How did youth culture change?

Possibly the greatest social change in the USA of the 1950s and the 1960s was the emergence of a distinct youth culture.

▶ The 1950s

The decade saw the emergence of the teenager and teenage rebellion. In the past young adults had simply imitated their parents' tastes and fashions and had been firmly kept in their place. The teenager of the 1950s seemed to want to rebel against everything and especially against whatever their parents believed in. They formed gangs, cruised in cars, drank heavily and attacked property.

In addition they developed their own identity as teenagers by wearing distinctive clothes and listening to their own music. Other young people 'dropped out' of conventional society altogether to become **beatniks**.

These changes were due to several factors.

● Young people in 1950s America had far more money to spend than previous generations of young people due to the country's increasing affluence, and companies responded with new products specifically targeted towards them. In 1957, it was estimated that the average teenager had $10–15 a week to spend, compared with $1–2 in the 1940s. Teenagers' annual spending power climbed from $10 billion in 1950 to $25 billion in 1959.

● They were the first generation to grow up under the shadow of nuclear war – it was a fear that nuclear weapons would destroy the world at the push of a button. The world could end at any time so teenagers wanted to enjoy 'today'.

● Many teenagers were influenced by the youth films of the 1950s. *Rebel Without a Cause* was the first film to appeal specifically to a teenage audience. As such, it was also the first film to address the issue of a **generation gap**. The film made a cult hero of

Source A A poster advertising the film *Rebel Without a Cause*

James Dean, the more so as he was killed in a car accident in 1955 aged only 24. In the film, Dean plays a character who rebels against his parents, even coming to blows with his father, and gets into trouble with the local police for drunkenness.

- Some American writers influenced the younger generation by questioning the cosy values of suburbia, such as J. D. Salinger in his novel *The Catcher in the Rye* (1951), which is about a high school dropout.
- The development of rock and roll music was crucial, for it gave teenagers music of their own to listen to, instead of having to listen to their parents' type of music. The more parents disliked the new music, the more popular it was with teenagers. In 1956, Elvis Presley erupted onto the pop music scene, singing songs that broke all sales records, such as *Heartbreak Hotel* and *Hound Dog*. He was a phenomenal success with teenagers, whilst their parents and teachers deplored his sensual style of performing, his tight jeans and his permanent sneer. He was the first rock and roll star to influence the young in their attitude to authority and their appearance. Moreover, he greatly popularised rock and roll music. Rock and roll grew and was transformed into many musical variations.

Elvis Presley

In the 1960s The Beatles, The Rolling Stones and other British groups took the United States by storm. 'Hard rock' grew popular, and protest songs, such as those by singer/songwriter Bob Dylan, became common. The Beach Boys were an American rock band, formed in 1961, who gained popularity for their close vocal harmonies and lyrics reflecting a Southern California youth culture of cars, surfing and romance.

Many white middle-class parents were shocked and concerned by their teenage children's explosion of anger and lack of respect for the law. It was claimed that rock and roll music encouraged teenage crime.

TASKS

1 Study Source A. What does it suggest about attitudes towards teenagers in the 1950s?

2 Explain why many teenagers rebelled against society in the 1950s.

Youth counterculture

The American youth continued to develop their own **counterculture** during the late 1950s and 1960s.

- Hair grew longer and beards became common. Blue jeans and T-shirts took the place of slacks, jackets, and ties.
- The use of illegal drugs increased.
- The introduction of the contraceptive pill seemed to encourage greater sexual freedom and promiscuity.

The hippy movement

Other young people protested in a totally different way. They decided to 'drop out' of society and become hippies. This meant they grew their hair long, wore distinctive clothes and developed an 'alternative lifestyle'. Often they travelled round the country in buses and vans and wore flowers in their hair as a symbol of peace rather than war. Their slogan was 'Make love, not war'.

Because hippies often wore flowers and handed them out to police they were called 'flower children'. They often settled in communes. San Francisco became the hippy capital of America. Their behaviour, especially their use of drugs, frequently led to clashes with the police who they nicknamed 'pigs'.

They were influenced by rock groups such as The Grateful Dead and The Doors. The high point of the movement came at the Woodstock rock concert at the end of the 1960s (see Source B). Woodstock was a three-day music festival in rural New York State in August 1969 attended by almost half a million people. The festival gave its name to the era, the Woodstock Generation.

This movement was of particular concern to the older generation because:

- Hippies often refused to work
- they experimented in drugs such as marijuana and LSD
- many were from middle-class and not under-privileged backgrounds. They rejected all the values that their parents believed in.

Source B A group of hippies wearing typical 'hippy' clothes, drumming together before the start of the Woodstock festival in 1969

Source C Jim Morrison, lead singer of the group The Doors, 1969

I like ideas about the breaking away or overthrowing of established order. I am interested in anything about revolt, disorder, chaos, especially activity that seems to have no meaning. It seems to me to be the road towards freedom – external freedom is a way to bring about internal freedom.

Popular music, 1970–2000

Popular music underwent many changes in the later twentieth century and was a key factor in influencing the culture of young Americans.

- In the 1970s disco performers such as Donna Summer, the Bee Gees, KC and the Sunshine Band, Chic, and the Jacksons became very popular. Disco was a reaction to the domination of rock music and was particularly popular with women. The disco became a favourite hang-out for teenagers, further popularised by the film *Saturday Night Fever* (1977).
- Rap and hip hop music developed, to a certain extent, from the disco music of the 1970s and became very popular in the last twenty years of the century. Although very much a product of

inner-city problem areas, especially those with high unemployment among young black Americans, research carried out on consumer groups during the mid-1990s highlighted the fact that over 75 per cent of hip hop record buyers were young and white. Hip hop had become popular and mainstream. Jay-Z's *Vol. 2 ... Hard Knock Life* album reached the US number 1 position for five weeks in 1998. Other artists/bands such as Ice T, Will Smith and the Fugees all achieved great chart success.

TASKS

3 Study Source C. What does it tell you about youth counterculture?

4 Describe the youth counterculture of the 1960s. (For guidance on how to answer this type of question, see pages 41–42.)

5 Look at Source A (page 48) and Source B (page 50) about youth culture. Explain why youth culture changed between the 1950s and 1960s. (For guidance on how to answer this type of question, see pages 60–62.)

Jay-Z in concert

What were the key features of the student movement?

In the 1960s students became heavily involved in the **civil rights movement** and the campaign for greater freedom of speech at universities, whilst many opposed US involvement in the conflict in Vietnam.

The swinging sixties
The attitudes of teenagers in the 1950s carried over to the next decade. It is often described as the 'swinging' sixties as the young distanced themselves even more from the older generation and its view of how the young should behave. They demanded greater freedom in everything they did: the music they listened to; the clothes they wore; the social life they led.

Protest singers
The 1960s saw an explosion in pop music which, in turn, was an expression of this emerging youth culture and of protest against important issues of the day. For example, Bob Dylan's lyrics covered the themes of the changing times – nuclear war, racism and the hypocrisy of waging war. Artists such as Jimi Hendrix, Janis Joplin and Joan Baez sang about sex, drugs and opposition to the war in Vietnam.

Universities
Many students wanted a greater say in their own education. They wanted to take part in running the universities and an end to college rules and restrictions imposed upon them. The 1960s were also a time of student protest across the world. For example, in the later 1960s there were student protests in Northern Ireland for civil rights for Catholics and in 1968 student demonstrations and strikes in Paris.

The SDS
One of the first student protest groups to emerge in the USA was the Students for a Democratic Society (SDS). It was set up in 1959 by Tom Hayden to give students a greater say in how courses and universities should be run. It had 100,000 members by the end of the 1960s. The SDS first achieved national prominence when, in 1964, it helped to organise the 'free speech movement' in the University of California at Berkeley. Up to half of Berkeley's 27,500 students took part in this campaign in 1964 and 1965. The SDS also played a key role in the protest movement against the war in Vietnam, including staging draft card burnings.

The influence of Martin Luther King
For many young Americans, white and black, their first experience of protest was in civil rights. Martin Luther King's methods proved inspirational and many white students supported the **freedom marches**, **freedom rides** and the **sit-ins** of the early and mid-1960s (see pages 84–89). Moreover, a disproportionate number of black American students were called up to fight in Vietnam. Influential black figures such as Martin Luther King spoke out against the war.

Involvement with civil rights
In 1964, student societies organised rallies and marches to support the civil rights campaign. Many were appalled at the racism in American society and were determined to expose racists in their own colleges: they demanded free speech.

The conflict in Vietnam
Many students were called up to the armed forces. This was known as the draft system. Opposition to the war grew with the number of casualties. In 1965 there were fewer than 2000 US casualties. By 1968 the number had increased to 14,000. Some students questioned the right of the USA to be in Vietnam. The USA was supporting a corrupt regime in South Vietnam. US methods of warfare brought even greater opposition, especially the use of chemical weapons such as napalm and the killing of innocent civilians such as at My Lai in 1968.

Anti-war protests
The anti-war protests reached their peak during 1968–70. In the first half of 1968, there were over a hundred demonstrations against the war, involving 400,000 students. In 1969, 700,000 people marched in Washington DC against the war. Students at these demonstrations often burned draft cards or, more seriously, the US flag which was a criminal offence. This, in turn, led to angry clashes with police. However, the most serious clash took place at Kent State University, Ohio, on 4 May 1970. National Guardsmen, called to disperse the students, used tear gas to try to move them. When they refused to move shots were fired. Four people were killed and eleven injured. The press in the USA and abroad were horrified and some 400 colleges were closed as 2 million students went on strike in protest against this action.

Source A A shocked student holds her head in disbelief as she looks at the body of one of the four students killed at Kent State University, Ohio, in 1970

Source B Part of President Richard Nixon's speech, 1 May 1970

You think of those kids out there [in Vietnam]. They are the greatest. You see these bums blowing up the campuses ... they are the luckiest people in the world, going to the greatest universities and here they are burning up the books, I mean storming around about this issue – get rid of the war. Out there [in Vietnam] we've got kids who are just doing their duty. They stand tall and they are proud.

Source C Arthur Krause, the father of one of the students who died at Kent State University, talking about his daughter on television, 5 May 1970

She resented being called a bum because she disagreed with someone else's opinion. She felt that our crossing into Cambodia was wrong. Is this dissent a crime? Is this a reason for killing her? Have we come to such a state in this country that a young girl has to be shot because she disagrees deeply with the action of her government?

▶ The importance of the student movement

In many respects, the most long-lasting achievement of the student movement was youth culture itself. By the end of the 1960s, there were profound changes in the whole lifestyle of the young. This was partly reflected in fashion, with the young becoming far more fashion-conscious and determined to move away from the 'norm' of the older generation. Perhaps the best example of this is the miniskirt, which was also a reflection of the greater **sexual permissiveness** of the era. Teenagers became much more aware of their individuality and demanded a greater say in what they wore and did.

Although the SDS and student protests did not bring an end to the war in Vietnam, there is no doubt that they helped to force a shift in government policy and make the withdrawal from Vietnam much more likely. They certainly influenced President Johnson's decision not to seek re-election in 1968.

In addition, the student movement provided greater publicity for the racism still prevalent in US society. The support of many white students for black civil rights strengthened the whole protest movement and showed that most American youths would no longer tolerate discrimination and segregation.

Finally, it should be remembered that the bulk of the students were of middle-class origin. They would have been expected to support the government in most areas. For such people to oppose the government on key issues (and in some cases oppose their families' views) was virtually unheard of and shook the older, more conservative generation.

TASKS

1 Make your own mind map to show the reasons behind the student movement.

- Rank in order the reasons clockwise from the most to the least important.
- Use different coloured pens to show links between some of the reasons.
- Briefly explain the links between the reasons.

2 Put together a headline in a national newspaper the day after the Kent State University deaths.

3 Look at Sources B and C (page 53) about student protest. Explain why events at Kent State University in 1970 changed the student protest movement. (For guidance on how to answer this type of question, see pages 60–62.)

4 Why was the era of the student movement a turning point in American social history? (For guidance on how to answer this type of question, see pages 75–76.)

5 Youth culture underwent great changes in the 1960s. Female fashion is one example. Research one other example and prepare a one-minute talk on its key changes. Here are some possible areas of research:

- US television for the young
- the film industry
- new dance crazes
- magazines and advertisements
- changes in male youth fashion
- protest singers.

How did the role of women in the USA change in the years after 1945?

There were important changes in the position of women in US society in the second half of the twentieth century.

▶ The impact of the Second World War

Before 1945, most American women had traditional roles as wives and mothers, with few women following careers. There were few real career opportunities except in typically 'female' professions such as teaching, nursing and secretarial work.

Source A A poster from wartime USA featuring Rosie the Riveter, 1942. Rosie was a fictional female worker used by the US government in a poster campaign to encourage women to help with the war effort. Hollywood even made a movie about Rosie

The Second World War had mixed results for the position of women.

- Women made a great contribution to the war effort and this opened up many new areas of employment for working-class women, especially in producing munitions. Indeed, the pay in munitions work was much higher than that normally paid to women in typically 'female' occupations. The number of women employed increased from 12 million in 1940 to 18.5 million, five years later. Many of these new jobs were in traditionally 'male' occupations such as the shipyards, aircraft factories and munitions.
- Women also joined the armed forces, with about 300,000 serving in the women's sections of the army, navy and the nursing corps.

Nevertheless, at the end of the war:

- the majority of women willingly gave up their wartime jobs and returned to their role as mothers and wives and their traditional 'female' jobs
- women were generally excluded from the highest, well-paid jobs and, on average, earned 50–60 per cent of the wage that men earned for doing the same job
- women could still be dismissed from their job when they married.

TASKS

1 Study Source A. What does it suggest about the role of women during the Second World War?

2 Describe the work of women during the Second World War. (For guidance on how to answer this type of question, see pages 41–42.)

▶ The 1950s

The Second World War had seen some progress in the position of women but, for the most part, this did not continue for the generation of women who followed. Indeed, there was much media influence encouraging women to adopt their traditional family role. Women who went out to work instead of getting married were treated with great suspicion by the rest of society.

Source B From *The Woman's Guide to Better Living*, written in the 1950s

> Whether you are a man or woman, the family is the unit to which you most genuinely belong. The family is the centre of your living. If it isn't, you've gone astray.

In the 1950s, growing numbers of women, especially those from middle-class backgrounds, began to challenge their traditional role as they became increasingly frustrated with life as a housewife. Moreover, the contraceptive pill gave females much greater choice about when or whether to have children. This could be prevented or postponed whilst a woman pursued her career.

Women were now much better educated so they could have a professional career. In 1950, there were 721,000 women at university. By 1960, this had reached 1.3 million. Moreover, the impact of labour-saving devices and convenience foods gave women more free time and this led some to seek paid employment. However, many of these women had a very limited choice of career because, once they married, they were expected to devote their energies to their husband and children.

Source D From the 1955 film *The Tender Trap*. A conversation between two of the leading characters in the film, Debbie Reynolds and Frank Sinatra

Reynolds: The theatre's all right, but it's only temporary.

Sinatra: Are you thinking of something else?

Reynolds: Marriage, I hope. A career is just fine, but it's no substitute for marriage. Don't you think a man is just the most important thing in the world? A woman isn't a woman until she's been married and had children.

Source C The typical 'mother' image from the 1950s

The 1960s

Despite post-war attitudes, the number of women in employment continued to increase as they were a valuable source of cheap, often part-time, labour for many employers. In 1950, women made up nearly 29 per cent of the workforce. By 1960, this was almost 50 per cent. Eleanor Roosevelt, the widow of President Roosevelt, made an important contribution to the cause when, in 1960, she set up a commission to investigate the status of women at work. Eleanor had been a keen supporter of women's rights since the 1920s. The report was published in 1963 and highlighted women's second-class status in employment. For example, 95 per cent of company managers and 85 per cent of technical workers were men. Only 7 per cent of doctors were women and, even less, 4 per cent, were lawyers. Women earned only 50 to 60 per cent of the wages of men who did the same job and they generally held low-paid jobs.

Another woman, Betty Friedan, was even more influential in the emergence of the women's movement. In 1963 she wrote *The Feminine Mystique*. Her book expressed the thoughts of many women – that there was more to life than being a mother and housewife. Indeed the expression 'the feminine mystique' was her term for the idea that a woman's happiness was all tied up with her domestic role.

Source E From *The Feminine Mystique* by Betty Friedan, 1963

The problem lay buried, unspoken for many years in the minds of American women. It was a strange stirring, a sense of dissatisfaction, a yearning that women suffered in the middle of the twentieth century in the United States.

Friedan was important because she encouraged women to reject this 'mystique' and called for progress in female employment opportunities. Disillusioned with the lack of progress in employment opportunities despite government legislation in 1963 and 1964 (see page 59), in 1966 she set up the National Organisation for Women (NOW).

National Organisation for Women (NOW)

This was set up by mainly white middle-class women in order to attack obvious examples of discrimination. By the early 1970s it had 40,000 members and had organised demonstrations in many American cities.

Its members challenged discrimination in the courts and in a series of cases between 1966 and 1971 secured $30 million in back pay owed to women who had not been paid wages equal to men.

Source F The Bill of Rights which was agreed at NOW's first national conference, 1967

1. Equal Rights Constitution Amendment
2. Enforce Law Banning Sex Discrimination in Employment
3. Maternity Leave Rights in Employment and Social Security Benefits
4. Tax Deduction for Home and Child Care Expenses for Working Parents
5. Child Day Care Centres
6. Equal and Unsegregated Education
7. Equal Job Training Opportunities and Allowances for Women in Poverty
8. The Right of Women to Control Their Reproductive Lives

TASKS

3. Study Source B. What view does it have about the role of women?

4. Look at Sources C and F about the lives of women in the 1950s and 1960s. Explain why attitudes towards the role and status of women had changed by the 1960s. (For guidance on how to answer this type of question, see pages 60–62.)

5. Working in pairs, write letters to a local newspaper from two American women who have read Betty Friedan's *The Feminine Mystique* in the mid-1960s:
   - one giving reasons in support of Friedan's views
   - one opposing them and giving the traditional view of women.

6. Study Source F. Which do you think are the **three** most important aims of NOW? Give reasons for your choices.

The Women's Liberation Movement

The Women's Liberation Movement was the name given to women who had far more radical aims than NOW. They were also known as **feminists** and were much more active in challenging discrimination. Indeed, the really extreme feminists wanted nothing to do with men. All signs of **male supremacy** were to be removed. These included male control of employment, politics and the media.

These women believed that even not wearing make-up was an act of protest against male supremacy and were determined to get as much publicity for their cause as possible. For example, they burned their bras as these were also seen as a symbol of male domination. In 1968, others picketed the Miss America beauty contest in Atlantic City (see Source G) and even crowned a sheep 'Miss America'. The whole contest, they argued, degraded the position of women.

However, the activities of the Women's Liberation Movement did more harm than good. Their extreme actions and protests brought the wrong sort of publicity. Burning their bras in public brought ridicule to the movement and made it increasingly difficult for men and other women to take the whole issue of women's rights seriously. They were a distraction from the key issues of equal pay and better job opportunities.

▶ Achievements of the women's movement

In recent years some women have broken into traditionally male dominated careers.

● In 1983, Dr Sally Ride became the first American woman in space on the shuttle Challenger (STS-7).
● In the 2008 presidential nomination race, Hillary Clinton won more primaries and delegates than any

Source G Members of the Women's Liberation Movement hold protest signs outside the Miss America pageant (contest) in Atlantic City, 7 September 1968

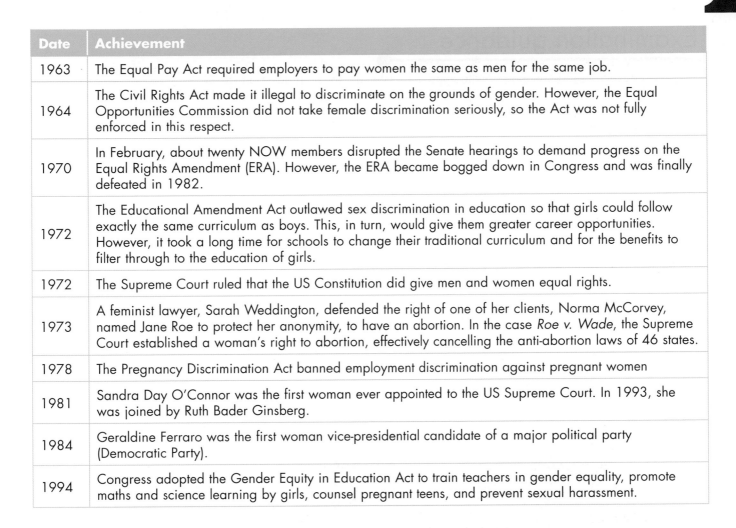

Date	Achievement
1963	The Equal Pay Act required employers to pay women the same as men for the same job.
1964	The Civil Rights Act made it illegal to discriminate on the grounds of gender. However, the Equal Opportunities Commission did not take female discrimination seriously, so the Act was not fully enforced in this respect.
1970	In February, about twenty NOW members disrupted the Senate hearings to demand progress on the Equal Rights Amendment (ERA). However, the ERA became bogged down in Congress and was finally defeated in 1982.
1972	The Educational Amendment Act outlawed sex discrimination in education so that girls could follow exactly the same curriculum as boys. This, in turn, would give them greater career opportunities. However, it took a long time for schools to change their traditional curriculum and for the benefits to filter through to the education of girls.
1972	The Supreme Court ruled that the US Constitution did give men and women equal rights.
1973	A feminist lawyer, Sarah Weddington, defended the right of one of her clients, Norma McCorvey, named Jane Roe to protect her anonymity, to have an abortion. In the case *Roe v. Wade*, the Supreme Court established a woman's right to abortion, effectively cancelling the anti-abortion laws of 46 states.
1978	The Pregnancy Discrimination Act banned employment discrimination against pregnant women
1981	Sandra Day O'Connor was the first woman ever appointed to the US Supreme Court. In 1993, she was joined by Ruth Bader Ginsberg.
1984	Geraldine Ferraro was the first woman vice-presidential candidate of a major political party (Democratic Party).
1994	Congress adopted the Gender Equity in Education Act to train teachers in gender equality, promote maths and science learning by girls, counsel pregnant teens, and prevent sexual harassment.

other female candidate in American history, but narrowly lost to Senator Barack Obama, who later appointed her as Secretary of State when he became President.

- Sarah Palin was chosen by Republican Party presidential candidate John McCain in August 2008 to be his running mate in that year's presidential election. She was the first female vice-presidential nominee of the Republican Party.

Moreover, there has been considerable progress in female employment. Over 70 per cent of women of working age were in employment in 1995 as compared to 38 per cent 40 years earlier. However:

- many of these were in traditional female occupations such as secretaries and receptionists. Only 30 per cent of managers were female
- over two-thirds of part-time jobs were done by women
- average women's earnings were about 75 per cent of those of men in 1998.

TASKS

7 Study Source G. What does it tell you about the Women's Liberation Movement?

8 Make a copy of the table below and list the achievements and limitations of the women's movement. Overall, was it a success? Explain your answer.

Achievements	Limitations

9 Why was the 1960s a turning point in the women's movement? (For guidance on how to answer this type of question, see pages 75–76.)

Examination guidance

This section provides guidance on how to approach tasks like those in question (b) in Unit 3. It requires you to identify and explain the extent of change and/or continuity in a key issue or development through the comparison of two sources and the use of your own knowledge. It is worth 7 marks.

Look at Sources A and B about lives of women in America between the 1950s and 1970s.

Source A A description of the ideal woman in *Life* magazine, 1956

A 32 year-old pretty and popular suburban housewife, mother of four, who had married at the age of sixteen, an excellent wife, mother, hostess, volunteer, and home manager who makes her own clothes, hosts dozens of dinner parties each year, sings in the church choir, and is devoted to her husband. In her daily round she attends club or charity meetings, drives the children to school, and does the weekly grocery shopping. Of all the accomplishments of the American woman the one she brings off with most spectacular success is having babies.

Source B Members of the Women's Liberation Movement demonstrating in August 1970

Explain why life had changed for some women by the 1970s. **(7 marks)**

[In your answer, you should use the information in the sources and your own knowledge to show the extent of change and the reasons for this.]

(Two different sample responses to this question are given on pages 61 and 62.)

Tips on how to answer

This question asks you to identify change or lack of change (continuity) and to use your own knowledge to help describe and explain this change or continuity, placing each source into context. To do this you need to:

- **describe** what is in each source, making use of the caption written immediately above each source

- **refer directly to each source**, for example 'Source A says ... This contrasts with Source B which shows ...'

- attempt to **cross-reference**, pointing out what is the same or different in each source

- remember to include **specific factual detail** from your own knowledge to help place each source in its historical context.

- Remember that if you only use your own knowledge and **do not specifically refer to the sources you cannot advance beyond half marks**.

- Ensure that you have described and explained both sources, **displayed a sharp focus on the key issue of change or continuity**, and supported this with your own knowledge of this topic.

Response by Candidate A

The lives of many American women had changed considerably by the 1970s. In the 1950s many women were housewives, and concentrated their time upon looking after the home and bringing up the children. They were expected to be a good mother and good wife. This was the life of the ideal suburban housewife. By the 1970s however, things had changed. The 1960s had seen the growth of the feminist movement and many became involved in the fight for equal rights and sexual equality. More women were entering university and obtaining jobs in the professions. Attitudes had changed and through their campaigns women were now playing a more active part in society and in the workplace.

> An informed answer but it lacks any mention of either source.

Comment on Candidate A's performance

This answer is based almost entirely upon the candidate's own knowledge. The sources have been used as a guide and are mentioned indirectly. The candidate hints at the reasons for change such as the growth of feminism and the fight for equal rights. However, as there is no specific mention of either Source A or Source B, the marks awarded will be confined to a low Level Two, scoring just under half marks.

Response by Candidate B

Source A describes the position of women in the 1950s as given in 'Life' magazine in 1956 and suggests that the stereotypical picture of a woman was that of a suburban housewife. The source says that women were expected to be good housewives, spending their time looking after the home, bringing up the children, and being a good mother and a supportive wife.

Source B contrasts sharply with *Source A* and shows that this lifestyle had changed by the 1970s. The 1960s saw the growth of female liberation organisations, and more women began to enter the workplace in search of careers. *Source B* shows members of the Women's Liberation Movement demonstrating in August 1970. The banners the women are carrying call for equal rights for women. Women were now demanding equal rights and sexual equality. Many were spending longer in education, going to university and getting good jobs in the professions.

These two sources show the change in attitude towards women that took place between the 1950s and the 1970s. As a result of the growth of the feminist movement shown in *Source B* women gained in status in society and advanced in the workplace. This was very different from the position of the suburban housewife shown in *Source A*.

Comment on Candidate B's performance

Candidate B has produced a structured and well informed answer. There is a clear attempt to explain and analyse the content of both sources, expanding upon points through the inclusion of own knowledge. There are attempts at cross-referencing and the concluding paragraph spells out what has changed and identifies a reason for this change. The answer matches the requirements of Level Three and is worthy of being awarded the maximum [7] marks.

4 Why was there so much racial inequality in the USA between 1930 and 1945?

Source A The lynching of Rubin Stacy in Florida, 1935. Stacy was seized from the custody of the sheriff's deputies for allegedly attacking a white woman

TASK

Study Source A. What does it show you about the treatment of black Americans during the 1930s?

Many people living in the USA in the 1920s and 1930s experienced racism and bigotry. During this period, there was a great deal of hatred towards black Americans and the growth of the **Ku Klux Klan** had shown that there was organised racism. Many black Americans moved from the South to the northern states during the 1920s and 1930s in search of jobs and a better life. However, there was continued discrimination and even by the end of the Second World War, their position had improved little.

This chapter answers the following questions:

● What was the position of black people in the 1930s?
● What was the NAACP?
● What was the Ku Klux Klan?
● What impact did the Depression and New Deal have on black Americans?
● What was the impact of the Second World War upon the black population?
● What was the impact of the war on the civil rights issue?

Examination guidance
Throughout this chapter you will be given the opportunity to practise different exam-style questions. You will be given guidance on how to approach tasks like those in question (c) in Unit 3. This requires you to make a judgement about a turning point or the importance or success of a particular event, movement or individual. It is worth 8 marks.

What was the position of black people in the 1930s?

▶ The Jim Crow laws

Black people had been brought to America as slaves in the seventeenth and eighteenth centuries. By the time slavery was ended in the 1860s, there were more black Americans than whites living in the southern states. White-controlled state governments, fearing the power of black Americans, introduced laws to control their freedom. These were known as the Jim Crow laws after a nineteenth century comedian's act which ridiculed black people.

The Jim Crow laws had become accepted across the USA in 1896 following the *Plessy v. Ferguson* court case. In this case, the Supreme Court upheld the Louisiana state law which required railway companies to have separate black and white railway carriages. The Supreme Court ruled that **segregation** was **constitutional** provided that there were equal facilities. This became known as the **'separate but equal'** doctrine.

The laws segregated blacks in schools, parks, hospitals, swimming pools, libraries and other public places. In the twentieth century, new Jim Crow laws were passed in some states so that there were segregated taxis, race tracks and even boxing matches. In 1940, there were no black police officers in the states of Mississippi, South Carolina, Louisiana, Georgia and Alabama.

▶ Literacy tests

Black people found it hard to get fair treatment and were seen as second-class citizens. They were often prevented from voting and had to pass literacy tests in order to do so. The literacy test was given to potential voters to prove that they could read and understand parts of the constitution. However, black Americans were frequently asked impossible questions and this prevented many in the South from voting until the 1960s.

▶ Living conditions

In the South black Americans were denied access to good jobs and a reasonable education. They were intimidated by whites who tried to control them through fear and terror. Even those who migrated north found that conditions were not much better. Black Americans were given low paid jobs and were the first to be laid off in bad times. They generally lived in squalid tenement ghettos. In New York and Chicago they often lived in poorer housing than whites and yet paid higher rents. They had poorer education and health services than whites. The majority of black Americans had not benefited from the economic boom of the 1920s.

▶ Improvements

Nevertheless, there were some improvements for black Americans, especially in the northern states. In Chicago and New York there was a growing black middle class. In Chicago, in 1930, black people boycotted department stores until they agreed to employ black assistants. Jazz brought fame to several black singers and musicians such as Louis Armstrong. The black neighbourhood of Harlem in New York became the centre of the Harlem Renaissance for black singers, musicians, artists, writers and poets. Black theatre attracted big audiences whilst black performing artists, including singers, comedians and dancers, were popular in clubs and musical shows.

A segregated theatre, Leland, Mississippi, 1937

The Scottsboro trials

However, the position of black Americans at this time is best highlighted by the Scottsboro trials which took place in the early 1930s.

On March 25, 1931, two white females claimed they were raped by some black American boys on the Chattanooga to Memphis freight train. One of the girls later admitted that she had not been assaulted but the boys were still found guilty. Eight of the nine boys who were prosecuted were found guilty and sentenced to death, commuted to 75 years' imprisonment. There were re-trials over a period of years and the case eventually went to the Supreme Court where the convictions were overturned. The last of the Scottsboro Nine was released in 1950. President Roosevelt was told that the prosecution's case was based on a 'mass of contradictions and improbabilities'.

TASKS

1 Explain why black Americans living in the southern states disliked the Jim Crow laws.

2 Describe the problems that black Americans faced if they moved north. (For guidance on how to answer this type of question, see pages 41–42.)

3 Study Source A. What does it tell you about the American legal system in the early 1930s?

4 How important were the Scottsboro trials? (For guidance on how to answer this type of question, see page 96.)

Source A Photograph of the jury at the 1932 Scottsboro trial

What was the NAACP?

William Du Bois and other black activists formed the **National Association for the Advancement of Coloured People** (NAACP) in 1909. It had its own magazine which du Bois edited until 1934. The aims of the NAACP were 'to make 1,000,000 Americans physically free from **peonage**, mentally free from ignorance, politically free from disenfranchisement, and socially free from insult.'

During the First World War, the NAACP promoted the involvement of black Americans in the US military. It successfully campaigned for black Americans to be commissioned as officers in the army and by the end of 1918, 600 black Americans had gained commissions. More than 700,000 registered for service in the army.

By 1919 the NAACP had 90,000 members in 300 branches. The NAACP challenged **white supremacy**, especially the segregation laws, and made black Americans much more aware of their civil rights, especially the right to vote. The NAACP also campaigned against the practice of **lynching** in the southern states. It investigated and publicised the number of lynchings. When the film *The Birth of a Nation* came out in 1915 (see page 67) the number of lynchings increased noticeably. The NAACP campaigned against the film and asked people to boycott it.

Although its attempts to secure federal anti-lynching legislation were unsuccessful, the Association's nationwide and interracial fight against lynching eventually helped reduce the annual number of lynchings in the United States. Despite constant campaigning, the NAACP was unable to pressure any president into introducing civil rights legislation.

Membership of the NAACP was never large, mainly because most black Americans' existence was defined by securing and keeping a job. In addition, there was virtually no tradition of black Americans being involved in politics.

In 1930, Walter White became the new leader of the NAACP. He was able to raise the profile of the NAACP but anti-lynching bills were rejected by the Senate in 1937 and 1940. Walter White encouraged blacks to challenge discrimination through the courts and he also challenged the unequal funding in education. The NAACP employed the black lawyer Thurgood Marshall to fight against segregation in education and he was able to secure equal salaries for teachers in many states across the country. The Supreme Court also decreed that blacks had the right to the same quality of graduate education as whites.

Source A From a report by a civil rights worker for the NAACP, early 1930s

A Negro in the Deep South who tried to register might lose his job or his credit. He might be beaten, have his house set on fire, or be killed. 'I don't want my job cut off', one man explained. Another was more blunt: 'I don't want my throat cut', he said.

During the 1930s, the NAACP began to focus on economic justice. After years of tension with white labour unions, the Association cooperated with the newly formed Congress of Industrial Organizations in an effort to win jobs for black Americans. Walter White was a friend and adviser to Eleanor Roosevelt, and he met her several times in attempts to convince President Roosevelt to outlaw job discrimination.

TASKS

1 What was the NAACP?

2 Study Source A. What information does it provide about the intimidation of black Americans in the 1930s?

3 How successful was the NAACP in its campaigns against segregation? (For guidance on how to answer this type of question, see page 96.)

What was the Ku Klux Klan?

The Ku Klux Klan (KKK) was set up in the 1860s by soldiers who had fought in the **American Civil War**. Its aim was to terrorise black people after emancipation. It died out in the years after 1870 but revived after the release of the film, *The Birth of a Nation*, in 1915. The film reinforced the idea of white supremacy and attracted huge audiences. After the First World War, membership of the Klan increased as a reaction to the influx of more foreign immigrants.

Source A A description of Klan activities in Alabama in 1929

A lad whipped with branches until his back was ribboned flesh … a white girl, divorcee, beaten into unconsciousness in her home; a naturalised foreigner flogged until his back was a pulp because he married an American woman; a Negro lashed until he sold his land to a white man for a fraction of its value.

Source B A Ku Klux Klan parade, 1926

The Klan members were WASPS (White Anglo-Saxon Protestants). They saw themselves as being superior to other races. They were also anti-communist, anti-Jewish, anti-Catholic and against all foreigners.

Klansmen dressed in white sheets and wore white hoods. This outfit was designed to conceal the identity of Klan members. The white colour symbolised white supremacy. Members carried American flags and lit burning crosses at their night-time meetings. The leader was known as the Imperial Wizard. Officers of the Klan were known as Klaliffs, Kluds or Klabees.

Many politicians in the South knew that if they opposed the Klan, they might not be elected to Congress. When campaigning for re-election in 1924, one Congressman said, 'I was told to join the Klan or else.' Membership of the Klan declined in the 1920s, following the imprisonment of its leader, D.C. Stephenson. However, the power of the Klan was still evident when, in 1946, 15,000 people marched to the Lincoln Memorial in Washington demanding that the organisation be made illegal.

TASKS

1 Study Source A. What information does it provide about the activities of the KKK?

2 Describe the activities of the KKK. (For guidance on how to answer this type of question, see pages 41–42.)

3 How important was the KKK in the southern states of America? (For guidance on how to answer this type of question, see page 96.)

What impact did the Depression and New Deal have on black Americans?

▶ The impact of the Depression

Source A From an interview with a black American in 1970, who lived through the 1930s, quoted in *Hard Times* by Studs Terkel, 1970

The Negro was born in depression. It didn't mean too much to him, the Great American Depression, as you call it. There was no such thing. The best he could be is a janitor [caretaker] or a porter or a shoeshine boy. It only became official when it hit the white man.

The Depression (see page 6–7) had a tremendous impact on black Americans. Two million black farmers and **sharecroppers** were forced off the land. If they went to the northern cities they found that unemployment among blacks was as high as 60 per cent. There were even white vigilante groups set up to prevent blacks from getting jobs. As unemployment increased whites were forced to take the menial jobs that had previously been taken by blacks and this only worsened the situation for black people.

▶ The impact of the New Deal

The New Deal (see pages 13–17) did not bring radical changes and huge improvements for black Americans.

Source B Evicted black sharecroppers, 1936

However, there was some progress. One key change was the inclusion of black Americans in the government. About 50 black Americans served in various branches of the Roosevelt administration – nicknamed the 'Black Cabinet'. The most famous was Mary McLeod Bethune who was Head of the Negro Affairs Division of the National Youth Administration. She became a prominent figure during the Roosevelt administration. Eleanor Roosevelt, the president's wife, helped to raise awareness of black problems and was a close friend of Bethune.

The number of black Americans employed by the government rose from 50,000 in 1933 to 200,000 in 1945. The New Deal provided 1 million jobs for black Americans and training for 500,000. The Public Works Administration (PWA) allocated funds for the construction of black hospitals, universities and housing projects. PWA building contracts also contained clauses requiring that the number of blacks hired be at least equal in proportion to the number of blacks in the local population. The Federal Emergency Relief Administration (FERA) and other relief agencies granted aid to 30 per cent of all black American families.

Black people began to shift their voting allegiance. Most had previously supported the Republicans but they now began to support Roosevelt's Democrats.

Source C From *Roosevelt's America, 1932–41*, J Traynor, 1987

The number of blacks on relief increased from about 18 per cent of the black population in October 1933 to almost 30 per cent in January 1935. Many blacks began to vote for Roosevelt because they felt that they owed their survival to him.

However, Roosevelt did little to eliminate unfair hiring practices and discriminatory job conditions and he failed to support anti-lynching bills. Some government agencies such as the Tennessee Valley Authority (TVA – see page 14) often refused to hire black workers. The TVA new model town of Norris would not allow blacks to live there. The Civilian Conservation Corps (CCC), not only paid black people lower wages than whites but forced them to live in segregated camps.

The New Deal's Agricultural Adjustment Act (AAA) attempted to raise disastrously low crop prices by authorising the federal government to pay farmers to grow fewer crops. These crop reduction subsidies enabled landlords to dispossess so many black American tenants and sharecroppers that the AAA was often referred to sarcastically as the 'Negro Removal Act'.

TASKS

1 Study Source A. What information does it provide about the impact of the Depression upon black Americans?

2 Study Source B. Design a newspaper headline showing the impact of the Depression on black sharecroppers.

3 What was the 'Black Cabinet'?

4 What reasons are given in Source C to explain why many black Americans voted for Roosevelt?

5 Why was the New Deal a turning point for black Americans? (For guidance on how to answer this type of question, see pages 75–76.)

6 Working in pairs, write a brief speech criticising the lack of help Roosevelt's New Deal policies gave to unemployed black workers.

What was the impact of the Second World War upon the black population?

▶ The Jim Crow army

The war highlighted the racism and discrimination in the armed forces, especially as the USA was fighting against a racist state, Nazi Germany. Many black Americans enlisted and formed the Jim Crow army. They were aware that they would have to serve in segregated units. It was only towards the end of the war that black servicemen saw much action.

● Black soldiers stationed in Britain were treated far better than back home. In the army, there were black-only units with white officers.
● Before 1944, black soldiers were not allowed into combat in the Marines.
● Black people were employed to transport supplies, or as cooks and labourers.
● Many black women served in the armed forces as nurses but were only allowed to treat black soldiers.
● The US Air Force would not accept black pilots. In each armed service, black Americans performed the menial tasks and found promotion difficult.
● When black soldiers were injured, only blood from black soldiers could be used; many whites felt that to mix blood would 'mongrelise' the USA.

Source A From a letter written in April 1944 by Corporal Rupert Timmingham to the magazine *Yank* about travelling in Texas with other black soldiers

> *We could not purchase a cup of coffee at a Texas railroad depot but the lunchroom manager said we black GIs could go on around the back to the kitchen for a sandwich and coffee. As we did, about two dozen German prisoners of war, with two American guards, came to the station. They entered the lunchroom, sat at the tables, had their meals served, talked and smoked. I stood on the outside looking on, and I could not help but ask myself why are they treated better than we are? Why are we pushed round like cattle? If we are fighting for the same thing, if we are to die for our country, then why does the Government allow such things to go on?*

Source B This 'prayer' appeared in a black newspaper in January 1943

> **Draftee's prayer**
> *Dear Lord, today*
> *I go to war:*
> *To fight, to die*
> *Tell me what for*
> *Dear Lord, I'll fight,*
> *I do not fear*
> *Germans or Japs,*
> *My fears are here.*
> *America.*

● Discrimination was worst in the navy, with black soldiers given the most dangerous job of loading ammunition onto ships bound for war zones. For example, in 1944 a horrific accident killed 323 people – most of them black sailors.
● The Tuskegee airmen (332nd Fighter Group – all black Americans) won great acclaim acting as fighter escorts for US bombers
● The 761st Tank Battalion also won acclaim in the Battle of the Bulge and received praise from General Patton. The battalion's nickname was the 'Black Panthers'.

▶ Progress

However, progress was evident as the US Supreme Commander, General Eisenhower, supported integrated combat units. By the end of 1944, black soldiers were fighting in these units (as seen during the **Battle of the Bulge**) and there were hundreds of black officers in the army and the Marines. There were also fighter squadrons of black pilots, although they were not allowed to fly in the same groups as whites and by the end of 1945 some 600 black pilots had been trained. By the end of the war, 58 black sailors had risen to the rank of officer.

Source C Black American soldiers in 1944, during the Second World War

De-segregation in the navy came in 1946 and the other services in 1948. By 1955, the army had changed from being one of the most segregated organisations in the country to the most successfully integrated.

Source D From *Citizen Soldiers* by Stephen Ambrose, 1997

The US army's chief historian concluded his wartime report in 1946 on the employment of Negro troops with these words: 'My ultimate hope is that in the long run it will be possible to assign individual Negro soldiers and officers to any unit in the Army where they are qualified as individuals to serve efficiently.'

TASKS

1 Study Source A. What does it tell you about the treatment of black American soldiers during the Second World War?

2 What message is the writer trying to put over in Source B?

3 Describe the contribution of black Americans to the US armed forces during the Second World War. (For guidance on how to answer this type of question, see pages 41–42.)

4 Look at Sources C and D about black American soldiers. Explain why the treatment of black American soldiers had changed by the late 1940s. (For guidance on how to answer this type of question, see pages 60–62.)

Black Americans and employment during the Second World War

Source E From *Mr Black Labour* by the historian D Davis, 1972, quoting the president of the North American Aviation Company in 1942

While we are in complete sympathy with the Negro, it is against company policy to employ them as aircraft workers or mechanics, regardless of their training, but there will be some jobs as janitors [caretakers] for Negroes.

Two female workers in the arms industry during the war

As more and more men were conscripted, job opportunities in factories for black American women and older black American men increased. Despite the valuable contribution these people made they were often treated poorly. A newspaper, the *Pittsburgh Courier*, created the 'Double V' campaign after readers began commenting on the second-class status of black workers during wartime. 'Double V' meant victory at home in terms of improved civil rights as well as victory abroad against fascism on the battlefield.

In 1941, A. Philip Randolph, a leading black American, sought to remove discrimination in the armed forces and the workplace. He organised a 'March on Washington' movement. President Roosevelt feared the possible consequences of the march and met Randolph to discuss the issues. Roosevelt issued Executive Order 8802 which stopped discrimination in industrial and government jobs and also set up the Fair Employment Practices Commission (FEPC). The FEPC could not force companies to employ black people, but it could use the threat of withdrawing government contracts to encourage them to do so.

During the war, over 400,000 black Americans migrated from the South to the USA's industrial centres. The number of black Americans employed in government service rose from 50,000 to 200,000 and by the end of the war there were more than 2 million black Americans involved in industry. The war also meant a broadening of opportunities for black American women. Many became nurses but were only permitted to help black American soldiers.

TASKS

5 Study Source E. What does it tell you about race relations in the USA during the Second World War?

6 Did the Second World War improve employment opportunities for black Americans? Copy the table below and complete the boxes, explaining your answers.

Yes, because …	No, because …

What was the impact of the war on the civil rights issue?

Source A An incident during the Detroit riots, June 1943. A black American is trying to run away from whites who had just assaulted him. The man on the left is a photographer

The Second World War period had seen some progress made by black Americans in employment and in the armed forces, and many blacks had become more active in campaigning for civil rights. However, discrimination and segregation remained a way of life in the southern states, whilst the migration of many black Americans to the industrial cities of the North had created greater racial tension.

This increase in racial tension led to race riots in 47 cities. The worst of these was in Detroit in June 1943 when 25 black people and nine white people were killed. More than 700 people were injured and there was $2 million worth of damage to property. In the same year, nine black Americans were killed in riots in Harlem, New York. There were also riots at nine black army training camps, where the soldiers resented their unequal treatment.

Awareness of discrimination and its injustice led to a growth in the membership of the National Association for the Advancement of Coloured People during the war – from 50,000 to 450,000. Many of the new members were professionals, but there were also many new urban workers.

A new organisation called the Congress of Racial Equality (**CORE**) was founded by James Farmer in 1942. CORE was inspired by the non-violent tactics of Mahatma Gandhi in India. It used the idea of sit-ins at cinemas and restaurants; this did lead to the end of segregation in some northern cities. There was increased interest in politics in the South among black Americans and the numbers of registered voters rose from 3 per cent to 12 per cent in the years 1940–47.

The issue of civil rights split the Democrats in the 1948 presidential election. Truman wanted to introduce a civil rights bill (which would ban **poll taxes**) and also proposed an anti-lynching bill which the **Dixiecrats** (southern Democratic Party politicians) rejected.

The situation by the end of the 1940s

President Truman's 'Fair Deal' programme had offered hope, but by the end of the 1940s only modest gains had been made by those seeking improved civil rights. Truman set up a Committee on Civil Rights in 1946, and though it recommended laws to prevent lynching, a permanent commission on civil rights and the prevention of segregation in housing, nothing was done. Republicans and the Dixiecrats (see page 73) continued to block reforms. The most important reform came when the armed forces were desegregated in 1948.

Nevertheless, because of their contribution during the war, black Americans were now better placed to demand their full rights as American citizens. Their plight was constantly recognised by President Truman who made countless speeches and though no new laws were introduced, he did raise the nation's awareness of the problems of civil rights.

Source B From Executive Order 9981, 26 July 1948

It is hereby declared to be the policy of the President that there shall be equality of treatment and opportunity for all persons in the armed services without regard to race, colour, religion, or national origin. This policy shall be put into effect as rapidly as possible, having due regard to the time required to effectuate any necessary changes without impairing efficiency or morale.

The confidence of the NAACP was sufficiently high by the late 1940s that it felt able to challenge some states about the education of black students. The NAACP was able to show that in some states students in white schools had more money spent on them than students in black schools. This eventually led to the key case of *Brown v. Board of Education of Topeka* in 1954 (see page 78). There was also some improvement in voter registration for black Americans in the 1940s. In 1940, 2 per cent of black Americans were registered to vote and by 1947, this had risen to 12 per cent.

Source C From a letter by Harry S. Truman, 18 August 1948, describing his revulsion at lynching

The main difficulty with the South is that they are living eighty years behind the times and the sooner they come out of it the better it will be for the country and themselves. I am asking for equality of opportunity for all human beings and, as long as I stay here, I am going to continue that fight. When the mob gangs can take four people and shoot them in the back and everybody in the country is acquainted with who did the shooting and nothing is done about it, that country is in a pretty bad fix ...

TASKS

1 Look at Source A (page 73) and Source B about the treatment of black Americans. Explain why civilian life had changed for some black Americans by 1948. (For guidance on how to answer this type of question, see pages 60–62.)

2 Create two newspaper headlines about the race riots – one from a southern Dixiecrat newspaper and the other from one supporting the NAACP and CORE.

3 Study Source C. What information does it provide on the attitude of President Truman towards civil rights?

4 How important was the Second World War in the fight for civil rights? (For guidance on how to answer this type of question, see page 96.)

Examination guidance

This section provides guidance on how to approach tasks like those in question (c) in Unit 3. This question requires you to make a judgement about a turning point or the importance or success of a particular event, movement or individual. It is worth 8 marks.

Why was the Second World War a turning point for black Americans? (8 marks)

(Two different sample answers to this question are given below and on page 76.)

Tips on how to answer

- The reference to 'turning point' in the question implies a **sharp change in the direction of policy**.

- The thrust of the question is **about change** and the **causes of that change**.

- You need to consider what came before the event mentioned in the question and compare this to what came afterwards, **noting the change and the reasons for that change**.

- You need to support your observations with **specific factual detail**.

- Remember that this question requires you to **provide a judgement**, giving specific reasons why you think this event was a turning point.

Response by Candidate A

During the Second World War black Americans fought in the army for the USA and those who weren't fighting were at home making a contribution to the war effort by working in factories. Blacks served in the army first by performing menial tasks but by the end of the war there were many black fighter pilots and black commanding officers. However, blacks and whites remained segregated throughout the war and came home afterwards to continued segregation. Blacks weren't happy with their lack of recognition. After the war more people became involved in the fight to end segregation. The civil rights movement was born.

Generalised comments, lacking specific factual detail.

Judgement which lacks support.

Comment on Candidate A's performance

The candidate provides an overview which hints at change but does not concentrate upon the key issue of it being a 'turning point'. Several points have been identified but they lack specific factual support. The answer demonstrates only a limited analysis of the key issue and tends to be descriptive rather than analytical and evaluative. It matches the criteria for Level Two and was worthy of receiving half marks [4].

Response by Candidate B

Following America's entry into the war in 1941 black Americans enlisted to play their part in the fight against Japan and Nazi Germany and they formed the Jim Crow army. They had to fight in segregated units. Most men in the army were used in non-combat military jobs, but some did get a chance to serve in the front lines. The Tuskegee Airmen won glory for providing fighter escorts for bombers over Germany. The 761st tank battalion made up of black soldiers saw action in Europe. On the home front black Americans made an important contribution to the war effort and by 1944 there were 2 million black workers in factories.

Good detail, spelling out the contribution of black Americans to the war effort.

The war caused a change of attitude towards the Jim Crow laws from many black Americans. Some veterans came back with a more militant attitude, believing that having fought for freedom overseas they now needed to fight for their own freedom at home. During the war membership of the NAACP increased from 50,000 to 450,000 as more black people began to question the segregation laws. As part of his 'Fair Deal' policy, President Truman established a civil rights committee in 1946 to examine violence against black Americans. He was successful in ending segregation in the armed forces.

Identifies the war as a reason for change.

Shows how the situation was changing immediately after the war.

In many respects the experience of the war years led to a growing sense of injustice by many black Americans and was therefore a turning point. It resulted in a rise of black resistance and this helped lay the foundations for the campaign for civil rights which emerged in the 1950s.

A clear judgement which addresses the key issue of a 'turning point'.

Comment on Candidate B's performance

The candidate has produced a detailed and well structured answer. Observations are supported with specific factual detail. The first paragraph outlines the contribution of black Americans to the war effort and the second paragraph shows how this brought about a desire for change. The third paragraph acts as a good conclusion in which there is a clear reference to 'turning point' and an attempt at a reasoned judgement. The answer meets the requirements of Level Four, providing an informed and accurate analysis and evaluation of the key issue which addresses the thrust of the question.

Now you have a go:

Why was the fight to end segregation on public transport a turning point in the civil rights movement? **(8 marks)**

5 Why was it difficult for black Americans to gain equal rights in the 1950s and 1960s?

Source A Police leading black schoolchildren into jail following their arrest for protesting against racial discrimination near Birmingham City Hall, 4 May 1963

TASK

Study Source A. What does it show you about race relations in the USA in 1963?

There was considerable progress in the search for improved civil rights during the 1950s and 1960s. In education, landmark cases such as *Brown v. Board of Education of Topeka*, Little Rock High School and James Meredith did remove segregation but there was often unwillingness on the part of many states to embrace the changes. There was progress in de-segregating transport after the Montgomery bus boycott and the freedom rides. However, no new laws were introduced to outlaw racial discrimination until the mid-1960s and many politicians and ordinary US citizens remained opposed to radical change.

This chapter addresses the following issues:

● What was the importance of *Brown v Topeka*?
● Why were Little Rock High School and James Meredith significant in the struggle for equal education?

● What were the causes of the Montgomery bus boycott?
● How were sit-ins used in the fight for equality?
● What was the importance of the freedom riders?
● What was the role and significance of Martin Luther King?
● What was the role and significance of Malcolm X?
● What was the role and significance of the Black Power movement?
● What was the role and significance of the Black Panther movement?

Examination guidance
Throughout this chapter you will be given the opportunity to practise different exam-style questions. You will be given guidance on how to approach tasks like those in question (c) in Unit 3. This requires you to make a judgement about a turning point or the importance or success of a particular event, movement or individual. It is worth 8 marks.

What was the importance of *Brown v. Topeka*?

In the 1950s, segregation was still a key feature of life for black Americans and they were still subject to what were known as the Jim Crow laws (see page 64).

The first case to challenge segregation in education did not originate in the South, but in Topeka, a town in the mid-west state of Kansas. Linda Brown's parents wanted her to attend a neighbourhood school rather than the school for black Americans which was some distance away. Lawyers from the **NAACP**, led by Thurgood Marshall, presented evidence to the Supreme Court stating that separate education created low self-esteem and was psychologically harmful. Moreover, the evidence also pointed out that educational achievement was restricted because of this policy. The process took eighteen months and the decision was announced on 17 May 1954. Chief Justice Warren of the Supreme Court gave a closing judgement (see Source A).

Some areas began to de-segregate and, by 1957, more than 300,000 black children were attending schools which had formerly been segregated. However, there were 2.4 million black southern children who were still being educated in Jim Crow schools (separate schools for black Americans). Moreover, there were many states, especially in the South, which took deliberate measures to keep separate schools. More than 100 senators and congressmen from the southern states signed the Southern Manifesto, a document that opposed racial integration in education.

Over the next two years, southern state legislatures passed more than 450 laws and resolutions which were aimed to prevent the *Brown* decision being enforced. Despite the decision of the Supreme Court and the open hostility to the *Brown* case, President Eisenhower did little to encourage integration. He was forced into action in 1957 by the events at Little Rock High School.

Source A From the closing judgement of Chief Justice Warren of the Supreme Court at the end of the *Brown v. Topeka* case

Separating white and coloured children in schools has a detrimental effect upon coloured children. The impact is greater when it has the sanction of the law; for the separating of the races is usually interpreted as denoting the inferiority of the Negro group ... We conclude that in the field of public education the doctrine of 'separate but equal' has no place. Separate educational facilities are inherently unequal.

▶ Problems after *Brown v. Topeka*

However, the *Brown v. Topeka* judgement did not specify how integration should be carried out – apart from a vague notion of 'at the earliest possible speed'.

TASKS

1 How important was the *Brown v. Topeka* case in the fight against segregation in education? (For guidance on how to answer this type of question, see page 96.)

2 Did the *Brown v. Topeka* case bring progress for the civil rights movement? Copy the table below and complete the boxes, explaining your answers.

Yes, because ...	No, because ...

Why were Little Rock High School and James Meredith significant in the struggle for equal education?

After the *Brown* v. *Topeka* decision, Little Rock High School, Arkansas, decided to allow nine black students to enrol. On 3 September 1957, the nine students, led by Elizabeth Eckford, tried to enter the school to enrol but were prevented by the state governor, Orval Faubus, who ordered National Guardsmen to block their entry. Faubus said there would be public disorder if black students tried to enrol. The following day, 4 September, the National Guard was removed by order of Faubus and the nine students ran the gauntlet of a vicious white crowd. At midday, the students went home under police guard because their safety could not be guaranteed. Press and television coverage in the USA and across the world was a serious embarrassment to a country which put itself forward as the champion of freedom and equality.

President Eisenhower had to act. He sent the 101st Airborne Division of over 1,000 federal troops to Little Rock to protect the black students for the rest of the school year. The 101st patrolled outside the school and escorted the black students into the school. In addition, each of the nine was assigned a personal guard from the 101st who followed them around the school to protect them from the white students. Despite the president's intervention, Faubus closed all Arkansas schools the following year, simply to prevent integration. Many white and most black students had no schooling for a year. Schools in Arkansas re-opened in 1959 following a Supreme Court ruling that schools must integrate.

TASKS

1 Study Source A. What does it show you about attitudes to integration in the USA in 1957?

2 Write a poem/protest song about events at Little Rock High School.

Source A Elizabeth Eckford again attempting to enter Little Rock High School, 4 September 1957

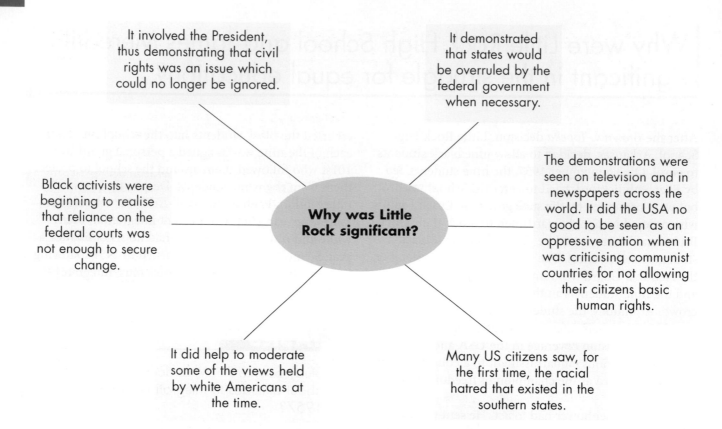

It involved the President, thus demonstrating that civil rights was an issue which could no longer be ignored.

It demonstrated that states would be overruled by the federal government when necessary.

Black activists were beginning to realise that reliance on the federal courts was not enough to secure change.

Why was Little Rock significant?

The demonstrations were seen on television and in newspapers across the world. It did the USA no good to be seen as an oppressive nation when it was criticising communist countries for not allowing their citizens basic human rights.

It did help to moderate some of the views held by white Americans at the time.

Many US citizens saw, for the first time, the racial hatred that existed in the southern states.

▶ The James Meredith case

In June 1962, the Supreme Court upheld a federal court decision to force Mississippi University to accept the black student James Meredith. The university did not want any black students and Meredith was prevented from registering. In his first major involvement in civil rights, President Kennedy sent in 320 federal marshals to escort Meredith to the campus. There were riots: two people were killed and 166 marshals and 210 demonstrators were wounded. President Kennedy then sent more than 2,000 troops to restore order. The black activists called the event 'The Battle of Oxford'. Three hundred soldiers had to remain on the campus until Meredith received his degree – three years later.

There were some other instances of resistance to integration in education, such as that led by Governor Wallace in Alabama when he tried to stop black Americans from enrolling at the state university. Wallace said, 'I am the embodiment of the sovereignty of this state, and I will be present to bar the entrance of any Negro who attempts to enrol at the university.' However, the fact that there had been federal intervention at Mississippi University showed that the tide had turned.

TASKS

3 Did events at Little Rock High School bring progress for the civil rights movement? Copy the table below and complete the boxes to explain your answers.

Yes, because …	No, because …

4 How important was education in the struggle for civil rights in the 1950s? (For guidance on how to answer this type of question, see page 96.)

5 Explain why the James Meredith case was important for the civil rights movement.

What were the causes of the Montgomery bus boycott?

Segregation on public transport in the USA had long been a problem for black Americans. There had been attempts to end this and there had been some success in the early 1950s in Baton Rouge, Louisiana. The issue came to a head in Montgomery, Alabama, after the arrest of Rosa Parks in December 1955. The rules about segregation on public transport in Montgomery were particularly harsh:

- Black Americans must follow the instructions of the white drivers.
- The front part of the bus is reserved for whites at all times.
- Black Americans must fill the bus from the back.
- Black Americans must not sit next to whites and must stand even if there is a vacant seat.
- If a white person boards the bus and all white seats are taken, blacks must give up their seats.

On 1 December 1955, Rosa Parks boarded a bus in the city of Montgomery and sat with three other black people in the fifth row – the first row that black people could occupy. A few stops later, the first four rows were filled with white people and one white man was left standing. According to the law black and white people could not share the same row, so the bus driver asked all four of the black people seated in the fifth row to move. Three of them moved; Rosa Parks refused.

Rosa Parks was subsequently arrested and from this point the situation escalated into a crisis. Initially, the Montgomery Women's Political Council, led by Jo Ann Robinson, decided to hold a one-day boycott of the buses on Monday 5 December, the day of Parks' trial. On the day after Parks' arrest, Robinson and some students printed thousands of leaflets encouraging people to boycott the city's buses.

Source A Part of the leaflet used to encourage the bus boycott, December 1955

Another Negro woman has been arrested and thrown in jail because she refused to get up out of her seat on the bus for a white person to sit down. This has to be stopped. Negroes have rights, too. This woman's case will come up on Monday. We are asking every Negro to stay off the buses Monday in protest of the arrest and trial. If you work, take a cab, or walk. But please, children and grown-ups, don't ride the bus …

Source B A cartoon published in the USA during the Montgomery bus boycott

TASK

1 What is the message of Source B?

Local civil rights activists such as Ralph Abernathy and Martin Luther King Jr (the new minister at Dexter Avenue Baptist Church) became involved. They held a meeting to plan a rally for the evening of the trial and the local NAACP began to prepare its legal challenge to the segregation laws. At the meeting, the **Montgomery Improvement Association** (MIA) was established to oversee the continuation and maintenance of the boycott and also to improve race relations. King was chosen to lead the MIA because he was quite new to Montgomery and the authorities knew little about him. It is thought that about 20,000 people were involved in the Monday boycott. During the evening of 5 December, some 7,000 attended the planned rally and heard Martin Luther King make an inspirational speech.

Rosa Parks was fined $10 for the offence on the bus and $4 costs. The MIA decided to continue the boycott until its demands were met. The Montgomery authorities then made a huge error of judgement, in refusing the moderates' demands. They pushed King and the MIA to demand complete de-segregation on buses.

Source C From the speech made by Martin Luther King, 5 December 1955

We are here this evening to say to those who have mistreated us so long that we are tired – tired of being segregated and humiliated, tired of being kicked about by the brutal feet of oppression. We have sometimes given people the feeling that we liked the way we were being treated. But we come here tonight to be saved from that patience that makes us patient with anything less than freedom and justice … in our protest there will be no cross burnings … We will be guided by the highest principles of law and order. Our method will be that of persuasion, not coercion.

What happened during the bus boycott?

Those boycotting the buses were helped during the first few days by black taxi companies. As the boycott progressed, churches bought cars in order to take people to and from work. This created problems because there had to be specific pick-up places for the workers and when people were waiting they were harassed by the police, who used local laws to try to prevent crowds gathering. Many drivers were arrested for minor traffic violations.

Despite their action, the boycotters faced continued intimidation. The Montgomery White Citizens Council led the organised opposition. Membership of this body swelled to almost 12,000 by March 1956, and its membership included some of Montgomery's leading city officials. In some cases the violence used against the boycotters was extreme. King and other leaders had their homes firebombed during 1956. The next step in intimidation came in February 1956, when about 90 of the leading figures, including King and Rosa Parks, were arrested for organising an illegal boycott. Though found guilty, no charges were made after appeal.

As the boycott moved into the summer of 1956, the US national press covered events more closely and this helped raise awareness of the issue of deep racial hatred in the South.

The MIA took the issue of segregation on transport to a federal district court on the basis that it was unconstitutional, citing the *Brown v. Topeka* case (see page 78). The federal court accepted that segregation was unconstitutional. However, the Montgomery city officials appealed and the case went to the Supreme Court. On 13 November 1956, the Supreme Court upheld the federal court's decision. The boycott had been successful. It formally came to an end on 20 December 1956 when King, Abernathy and other leaders travelled on an integrated bus.

TASKS

2 Study Sources A (page 81) and C. What arguments are being put forward by the activists to undertake a boycott and push for de-segregation on the buses?

3 Devise some slogans to encourage black Americans living in Montgomery in 1955 not to use the public buses.

▶ What was the importance of the bus boycott?

The bus boycott was important because:

- it showed that unity and solidarity could win
- victory offered hope to those who were fighting for improved civil rights
- the NAACP was vindicated in making a legal case and using the *Brown* case (see page 78) as a precedent
- it highlighted the benefits of a peaceful approach and, above all, showed that black Americans were able to organise themselves
- it brought King's philosophy to the fore and gave the movement a clear moral framework
- success encouraged King to consider further action which would confront inequality and bring about further change.

TASKS

4 Study Source D. What does it tell you about the Montgomery bus boycott?

5 Describe the events of the Montgomery bus boycott of 1955–56. (For guidance on how to answer this type of question, see pages 41–42.)

6 Write a newspaper article in support of the boycott.

7 Look at Source A (page 81) and Source E which are about public transport in the 1950s. Explain why travel on public transport for black Americans had changed by late 1956. (For guidance on how to answer this type of question, see pages 60–62.)

Source D
Montgomery citizens walking to work during the boycott

Source E Rosa Parks (middle) riding at the front of a bus after the end of the boycott

How were sit-ins used in the fight for equality?

The profile of the civil rights movement had been raised by events such as Montgomery and Little Rock and was raised even further by a series of sit-in protests which started in Greensboro, North Carolina in early 1960.

On 1 February 1960 four black students from a local college walked into a F.W. Woolworth store in Greensboro and demanded to be served at a whites-only lunch counter. On being refused they remained seated at the counter until the shop closed. The next day, they were accompanied by 27 more students and the day after a further 80 joined them. By the fifth day there were 300 students. The shop agreed to make a few concessions but the students later resumed their protests – some were now arrested for trespass. The students then boycotted any shop in Greensboro which had segregated lunch counters.

Sales immediately dropped and eventually segregation ended.

By August 1961 the sit-ins had attracted over 70,000 participants and resulted in over 3,000 arrests. The technique of the sit-ins was used to allow black people to use other public facilities such as movie theatres. This **direct action** led activists to challenge the deep-rooted racism of the South even further in what became known as the 'freedom rides'.

TASK

Describe the sit-in protests of the early 1960s. (For guidance on how to answer this type of question, see pages 41–42.)

Source A A sit-in protest at a 'whites only' lunch counter in Jackson, Mississippi

What was the importance of the freedom riders?

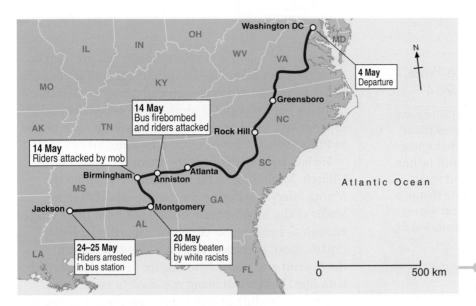

Map of the freedom rides, 1961

The Supreme Court decided in December 1960 that all bus stations and terminals that served interstate travellers should be integrated. The Congress of Racial Equality (CORE) wanted to test that decision by employing the tactic of the freedom ride. If there was continued failure to carry out the law, CORE would be able to show that narrow-mindedness and racism still existed in the southern states.

The first of the freedom rides began in May 1961 when James Farmer, the National Director of CORE, and twelve volunteers left Washington DC by bus to travel to New Orleans. The black Americans used whites-only facilities to ensure integration was taking place. There was little trouble on the first part of the journey. However, at Anniston, Alabama, a bus was attacked and burnt. In Montgomery, white racists beat up several of the freedom riders. In Jackson, Mississippi, 27 freedom riders from the **Student Non-violent Coordinating Committee** (SNCC) and **Southern Christian Leadership Conference** (SCLC) were jailed for 67 days for sitting in the whites-only section of the bus station.

When the freedom riders reached Birmingham, Alabama, there was no protection for them and they were attacked by an angry mob – the police chief ('Bull' Connor) had given most of the police the day off. Events at Jackson forced the new president,

John F. Kennedy, to intervene. Kennedy secured a promise from the state senator that there would be no mob violence. However, when the riders arrived in Jackson, they were immediately arrested when they tried to use the whites-only waiting room.

The freedom riders continued throughout the summer and more than 300 of them were imprisoned in Jackson alone. Attacks on them by the Ku Klux Klan increased. The Attorney General, Robert Kennedy, did not wish to see the situation escalate and was hoping that he would not have to send in US marshals to enforce the law. Violence was avoided in Mississippi when it became clear that marshals would be used. On 22 September the Interstate Commerce Commission issued a regulation that ended racial segregation in bus terminals.

TASK

1 Describe what happened on the freedom rides. (For guidance on how to answer this type of question, see pages 41–42.)

2 How successful were the sit-in protesters and the freedom riders? (For guidance on how to answer this type of question, see page 96.)

What was the role and significance of Martin Luther King?

Source A From the Nobel Peace Prize citation for Martin Luther King, 1964

He is the first person in the Western world to have shown us that a struggle can be waged without violence. He makes the message of brotherly love a reality in the course of his struggle, and he has brought this message to all nations and races. He has never abandoned his faith in the struggle he is waging, he has been imprisoned on many occasions, his family has been threatened, but he has never faltered.

Biography   Martin Luther King 1929–1968

1929 Born 15 January
1951 Graduated from Crozer Theological College with a degree in theology
1953 Married Coretta Scott
1955 Led Montgomery bus boycott
1957 Formed and led Southern Christian Leadership Conference
1963 'I have a dream' speech. Voted 'Man of the Year' by *Time* magazine
1964 Winner of the Nobel Peace Prize
1968 April 4, assassinated in Memphis

King was the son of a Baptist minister and grew up in a middle-class home in Atlanta, Georgia. As a teenager he spoke in his father's church and demonstrated that he had a gift for popular speaking. However, he had experienced racial prejudice as a student in such places as Philadelphia, New Jersey and Boston.

He had been minister at the Dexter Avenue Baptist Church, Montgomery, for less than a year when the Montgomery bus boycott began. He was chosen as leader of the MIA because he had not been there long enough to become too close to any particular local organisation. He was energetic and enthusiastic in the boycott and was able to inspire those who worked with him. His idea of using non-violent tactics was similar to Gandhi's in India and soon there were many civil rights activists keen to follow and copy King. His devout religious beliefs and unwavering faith won him many supporters. He was never intimidated. Martin Luther King helped to found the Southern Christian Leadership Conference (SCLC) after the bus boycott. The SCLC was black-led and black-run. King and many members of the SCLC felt that boycotts and other forms of non-violent protest should be adopted in the struggle for equality. The SCLC tried to increase the number of black voters with the 'Crusade for Citizenship'. This failed. Nevertheless, King had become the leading figure in the civil rights movement by 1963.

TASKS

1 Use the information in Source A to explain why Martin Luther King was awarded the Nobel Peace Prize in 1964.

2 Why was it significant that the SCLC was 'black-led and black-run'?

3 Describe Martin Luther King's career up to the early 1960s. (For guidance on how to answer this type of question, see pages 41–42.)

Martin Luther King and the Birmingham march, 1963

The civil rights issue exploded in 1963. There was still no federal law which made southern states integrate public facilities. In order to avoid de-segregating its parks, playgrounds and swimming pools, the city of Birmingham, Alabama, simply closed them all. King and the SCLC sought to challenge the city by using sit-ins and marches to press for de-segregation. It was hoped that this would achieve maximum publicity across the USA. Birmingham had a population of about 350,000, of which about 150,000 were black Americans. King hoped to mobilise a large part of them in the planned demonstrations.

Demonstrations began in April 1963 after some activists were arrested. Police Chief Eugene 'Bull' Connor then closed all public parks and playgrounds. This prompted King to address a large rally at which he said it was better to go to jail in dignity rather than just accept segregation. King was then arrested in a further demonstration and jailed for defying a ban on marches. During his short stay in prison, he wrote 'Letter from Birmingham Jail' (see Source B). This letter became one of the most famous documents of the civil rights movement.

The situation worsened on King's release from jail when it was decided to use children and students in the demonstrations to test the police reaction. On 3 May, Connor allowed his men to set dogs on the protesters and he then called in the fire department to use powerful water hoses. Connor arrested 2,000 demonstrators as well as almost 1,300 children. Television witnessed the events which were seen not only across the USA but also all over the world. Photographs of the demonstration and police reaction were published in national newspapers. This gave King all the publicity he wanted. It showed the violence of the authorities in the face of peaceful demonstrators. By early May there was chaos in Birmingham.

At this stage President Kennedy became involved. He sent the Assistant Attorney General, Burke Marshall, to mediate between the parties. Talks between King and the Birmingham city leaders resulted in a settlement on 9 May and it was agreed that de-segregation in the city would take place within 90 days.

A consequence of the violence was Kennedy's decision to bring in a Civil Rights Bill. On the same day, Medgar Evers, leader of the Mississippi NAACP, was shot dead in Jackson by a white sniper.

Source B Part of King's 'Letter from Birmingham Jail'

... our direct action program could be delayed no longer ... For years, I have heard the word 'Wait!' It rings in the ear of every Negro with piercing familiarity. This 'Wait!' has almost always meant 'Never'. We must come to see that justice too long delayed is justice denied. The nations of Asia and Africa are moving with jet-like speed toward gaining political independence, but we still creep at horse and buggy pace toward gaining a cup of coffee at a lunch counter.

Source C Police dogs attacking civil rights demonstrators in Birmingham, Alabama, 3 May, 1963

TASKS

4 Explain why events in Birmingham were important in the campaign for civil rights.

5 Study Source B. Why is King's 'Letter from Birmingham Jail' so important in the history of the civil rights movement?

6 Study Source C. What does it show you about police methods in Birmingham?

▶ Martin Luther King and the march on Washington, 1963

Why was the march held?

After Birmingham, the civil rights groups wanted to maintain their high profile and the idea of a march on Washington DC was put forward by Philip Randolph (see page 72). The NAACP, CORE, SNCC and SCLC all took part in organising the march. King was keen to have the march because he knew that there were those who felt that progress was slow and he worried that these people might drift towards violence if the high profile was not sustained. The Washington police put a hold on leave for its 3,000 officers in case there was violence. President Kennedy, fearing violence, asked the organisers to call off the march.

The march began as a call for jobs and freedom, but it broadened to cover the aims of the whole of the civil rights movement. There was naturally a demand for the passage of Kennedy's Civil Rights Bill.

The march

When the march took place, on 28 August 1963, there were about 250,000 demonstrators. The organisers had expected less than half this figure. People came from all over the USA. When politicians were seen, there were chants of 'Pass the bill' (referring to Kennedy's Civil Rights Bill). King was the final speaker of the day and his speech has now become part of the lore of the struggle for civil rights (see Source D).

Source D From King's speech in Washington DC, 28 August 1963

I have a dream. It is a dream deeply rooted in the American dream. I have a dream that one day this nation will rise up and live out the true meaning of its creed – we hold these truths to be self-evident, that all men are created equal …

I have a dream one day that on the red hills of Georgia, sons of former slaves and sons of former slave owners will be able to sit down together at the table of brotherhood …

I have a dream that my four little children will one day live in a nation where they will not be judged by the colour of their skin but by the content of their character. I have a dream today!

Martin Luther King at the Lincoln Memorial, 28 August 1963

The march on Washington was hailed as a great success. It was televised across the USA and did much for the civil rights movement. It brought together different sections of US society and put further pressure on President Kennedy to move forward on civil rights.

After the march, King and the other leaders met President Kennedy to discuss civil rights legislation. Kennedy was keen to let them know of his own commitment to the Civil Rights Bill. However, all at the meeting were aware that there were many Republican politicians still opposed to any changes.

King's hopes began to seem illusory. In September 1963 four black girls were killed in a bomb attack while attending Sunday school in Birmingham. The civil rights movement seemed to stall in late 1963 and was then hit by the assassination of President Kennedy.

The new President, Lyndon Johnson, pushed Kennedy's Civil Rights Bill through Congress and it became law in 1964. However, it did not guarantee black Americans the vote, so, in 1965, King decided to hold another non-violent campaign at Selma, Alabama (see pages 98–99). He decided to hold a march from Selma to Birmingham, to present a petition demanding voting rights. The marchers were attacked by police and state troopers. This became known as 'Bloody Sunday'. In response to this, on 15 March, President Johnson, in a speech to Congress, called for passage of a Voting Rights Act that would enfranchise black Americans. The Act was passed in August 1965: King's policy of non-violence had worked. After 1965, King broadened his work and moved to the North to help the poor black Americans. He also became prominent in the anti-Vietnam War movement and the 'Poor People's Campaign'.

▶ Martin Luther King's assassination

Source E From a speech given by King at a church rally, 3 April 1968, about his hopes and fears for the future

We've got some difficult days ahead. But it doesn't matter with me now. Because I've been to the mountain top. I may not get there with you, but I want you to know tonight ... that we as a people will get to the promised land!

The day after giving the speech in Source F, on 4 April 1968, Martin Luther King was in Memphis. He was visiting Memphis because he was supporting black refuse collectors who were striking for equal treatment with their white co-workers. The economic and educational gulf between blacks and whites was still great not only in the South but in the North. King was assassinated on that same day in Memphis. James Earl Ray, a white racist, was arrested and jailed for the crime, but there is still doubt over whether he was the real killer.

On his death, there was a final outburst of rioting across the country. Forty-six people died; more than 3,000 were injured in violent clashes and demonstrations across more than one hundred cities. This was a great irony – it seemed as if King's whole work and life had been for nothing.

TASKS

7 Explain why the march on Washington took place in August 1963.

8 Can you suggest reasons why King's 'I have a dream' speech (Source D) has become one of the most famous in history?

9 Study Source E. What did King mean when he said 'we as a people will get to the promised land!'?

10 Explain why the assassination of Martin Luther King resulted in a wave of rioting across the USA.

What was the role and significance of Malcolm X?

▶ Malcolm X and the Nation of Islam

For some in the civil rights movement, progress had been painfully slow and a feeling grew that Martin Luther King's methods would never bring equality in politics and equality of opportunity in life. A group which had never accepted King's ideas was the Nation of Islam (or Black Muslims) – its supporters openly sought separatism. Members rejected their slave surnames and called themselves 'X'.

The most famous member of the Nation of Islam was Malcolm X, and his brilliant oratory skills helped to increase membership to about 100,000 in the years 1952–64. He was a superb organiser and during the time he was a member of the Nation of Islam, he travelled across the USA winning converts. Malcolm X helped to set up educational and social programmes which were aimed at black youths in ghettos. By 1960, more than 75 per cent of the membership of the Nation of Islam was aged between 17 and 35. He is credited with re-connecting black Americans with their African heritage and is responsible for the spread of Islam in the black community in the United States. His influence on people such as Stokely Carmichael (see page 92) was crucial.

Many members of the mainstream civil rights groups did not like the Nation of Islam and some felt that the Muslims had a 'hate-white doctrine' which was as dangerous as any white racist group. Thurgood Marshall (see pages 32 and 66) said that the Nation of Islam was run by a 'bunch of thugs organised from prisons and financed by some Arab group'. Such criticism never concerned Malcolm X and he was never afraid to attack King and other leaders of the civil rights movement. He criticised the 1963 march on Washington, which he called 'the farce on Washington'. He could not understand why so many black people were impressed by 'a demonstration run by whites in front of a statue of a president who has been dead for a hundred years and who didn't like us when he was alive'.

Biography Malcolm X, born Malcolm Little, 1925–65

1925 Born 19 May in Omaha
1931 Father was murdered by white supremacists
1942 Lived in New York, involved in pimping and drug dealing
1946 Found guilty of burglary and imprisoned
1952 Released from jail. Had become a follower of the Nation of Islam. Changed his name to 'X'
1958 Married Betty Shabazz
1964 Left the Nation of Islam and formed Muslim Mosque, Inc. and the black nationalist Organisation of Afro-American Unity
1964 Went on pilgrimage to Mecca. His political and religious views altered. Changed his name to Malik El-Hajj Shabazz
1965 21 February, shot by three members of the Nation of Islam

Source A From a speech by Malcolm X in New York, 12 December 1964

I believe in the brotherhood of man, all men, but I don't believe in brotherhood with anybody who doesn't want brotherhood with me. I believe in treating people right, but I'm not going to waste my time trying to treat somebody right who doesn't know how to return the treatment.

Source B From Malcolm X's speech at the Founding Rally of the Organisation of Afro-American Unity, 28 June 1964

We have formed an organisation known as the Organisation of Afro-American Unity which has the same aim and objective to fight whoever gets in our way, to bring about the complete independence of people of African descent here in the Western Hemisphere, and first here in the United States, and bring about the freedom of these people by any means necessary. That's our motto. We want freedom by any means necessary. We want justice by any means necessary. We want equality by any means necessary.

◗ The influence of Malcolm X

Malcolm X had a tremendous influence on young urban black Americans. He felt that violence could be justified not only for self-defence but also as a means to secure a separate black nation. However, after a visit to Mecca he changed his views and left the Black Muslims to set up the Muslim Mosque, Inc. and the Organisation of Afro-American Unity to promote closer ties between Africans and African-Americans. Malcolm X said the trip to Mecca allowed him to see Muslims of different races interacting as equals. He came to believe that Islam could be the means by which racial problems could be overcome. He pushed to end racial discrimination in the USA, but this brought him enemies and he was assassinated by three black Muslims in February 1965.

Malcolm X's views and ideas became the foundation of the more radical civil rights movements such as Black Power (see pages 92–93) and the Black Panthers (see pages 94–95). Many historians have said that Malcolm X helped raise the self-esteem of black Americans more than any other individual in the civil rights movement.

TASKS

1 Why did Malcolm choose the name 'X'?

2 Describe the work of Malcolm X in the 1950s. (For guidance on how to answer this type of question, see pages 41–42.)

3 Study Source A. What does it tell you about Malcolm X's attitude to racism?

4 Explain why Malcolm X attracted the support of young black Americans.

5 Study Source B. What methods does Malcolm X suggest using to bring about change in the position of black Americans?

6 How important was Malcolm X in the campaign for civil rights? (For guidance on how to answer this type of question, see page 96.)

What was the role and significance of the Black Power movement?

Despite the progress of the late 1950s and early 1960s, many young black Americans were frustrated, and those who lived in the ghettos felt anger at the high rates of unemployment, continuing discrimination and poverty which they experienced.

▶ The Black Power movement

Out of this frustration the Black Power movement emerged. Black Power was originally a political slogan but it came to cover a wide range of activities in the late 1960s which aimed to increase the power of blacks in American life. Stokely Carmichael and others in the SNCC (see page 85) wanted blacks to take responsibility for their own lives and to reject white help. Carmichael and his followers wanted blacks to have pride in their heritage and they adopted the slogan 'Black is beautiful'. They wanted black Americans to develop a feeling of black pride and promoted African forms of dress and appearance.

Carmichael attracted criticism because of his aggressive attitude and was attacked when he denounced the involvement of the USA in the Vietnam War. He eventually left SNCC and became associated with the Black Panthers but left the USA and moved to Guinea in 1969 where he lived until his death in 1998.

Source A From a speech made in 1966 by Stokely Carmichael, leader of the SNCC, describing his own frustrations and those of many black Americans. He had just been released from police custody following involvement in a civil rights march in Mississippi

This is the twenty-seventh time I have been arrested. I ain't going to jail no more. The only way we gonna stop them white men from whuppin' us is to take over. We been saying freedom for six years and we ain't got nothin'. What we gonna start sayin' now is Black Power!

Biography Stokely Carmichael 1941–1998

1941 Born in Port of Spain, Trinidad and Tobago
1943 Moved to New York City
1960 Attended Howard University, Washington DC. Gained a degree in Philosophy
1961 Took part in the freedom rides; jailed for seven weeks
1966 Chairman of SNCC
1966 27th arrest; made his 'Black Power' speech
1967 Wrote *Black Power*
1968 Joined Black Panthers
1969 Left the USA and moved to Guinea. Changed his name to Kwame Ture
1998 Died in Guinea

Source B Tommie Smith and John Carlos at the 1968 Olympic Games in Mexico City. Smith won the gold medal and Carlos the bronze in the 200 metres. The silver medallist, Peter Norman (left), wears a badge to show his support for the Americans

The Black Power movement gained tremendous publicity at the 1968 Mexico City Olympics, at the winners' ceremonies for the Men's 200 metres and 400 metres relay. (See Source B). The athletes wore part of the movement's uniform – a single black glove and black beret – and also gave the clenched fist salute. During the ceremony, when the US national anthem was being played, Tommie Smith gave the salute with his right hand to indicate Black Power and John Carlos with his left to show black unity. Smith also wore a black scarf to represent black pride and black socks with no shoes to represent black poverty in racist America. Smith and Carlos were sent back to the USA. They were accused of bringing politics into sport and damaging the Olympic spirit. On their return, they both received several death threats.

Peter Norman, the Australian who came second in the 200 metres, also showed his support for the Black Power cause by wearing an OPHR (Olympic Project for Human Rights) badge. The Australian Olympic Committee was furious at his actions and did not select him for the 1972 Olympics. Norman died on 3 October 2006 and both Tommie Smith and John Carlos gave eulogies and were pallbearers at his funeral.

As a result of these athletes' actions, the whole world was now aware of the Black Power movement.

TASKS

1 What information does Source A give about the beliefs of Stokely Carmichael?

2 Describe the Black Power movement. (For guidance on how to answer this type of question, see pages 41–42.)

3 How important was Stokely Carmichael in the struggle for civil rights? (For guidance on how to answer this type of question, see page 96.)

4 Working in pairs, prepare a case to support and a case to condemn the actions of US athletes at the Mexico City Olympics in 1968.

What was the role and significance of the Black Panther movement?

Bobby Seale, left, and Huey Newton, co-founders of the Black Panther Party for Self Defence

At the same time as the urban riots and the development of 'Black Power', there emerged the 'Black Panthers'. This party was founded by Huey Newton and Bobby Seale in October 1966 in Oakland, California. Both men had been heavily influenced by Malcolm X. The Panthers had a ten-point programme and were prepared to use revolutionary means to achieve these aims.

The Black Panthers were even prepared to form alliances with radical white groups if it was felt it would help bring down the 'establishment'. The leaders of the Panthers advocated an end to capitalism and the establishment of a socialist society. Seale constantly stated: 'We believe our fight is a class struggle and not a race struggle.'

The Panthers wore uniforms and were prepared to use weapons, training members in their use. By the end of 1968, they had 5,000 members. However, internal divisions and the events of 1969, which saw 27 Panthers killed and 700 injured in confrontations with the police, saw support diminish. They were constantly targeted by the FBI and by 1982, the party had disbanded.

Source A The symbol of the Black Panther Party

Source B The Black Panthers' ten-point programme, October 1966

We want:

1. Freedom. We want power to determine the destiny of our Black Community.

2. We want full employment for our people.

3. We want an end to the robbery by the white man of our Black Community.

4. We want decent housing, fit for shelter of human beings.

5. We want education for our people that exposes the true nature of this decadent American society. We want education that teaches us our true history and our role in the present-day society.

6. We want all black men to be exempt from military service.

7. We want an immediate end to police brutality and murder of black people.

8. We want freedom for all black men held in federal, state, county and city prisons and jails.

9. We want all black people when brought to trial to be tried in court by a jury of their peer group or people from their black communities, as defined by the Constitution of the United States.

10. We want land, bread, housing, education, clothing, justice and peace.

Source C J. Edgar Hoover, FBI Director, quoted in the *New York Times*, 9 September 1968

The Black Panthers are the greatest threat to the internal security of the country. Schooled in communist ideology and the teaching of Chinese Communist leader Mao Tse-tung, its members have perpetrated numerous assaults on police officers and have engaged in violent confrontations with police throughout the country. Leaders and representatives of the Black Panther Party travel extensively all over the United States preaching their gospel of hate and violence not only to ghetto residents, but to students in colleges, universities and high schools as well.

During the 1950s and 1960s, tremendous progress had been made in many areas, especially education and transport. Legislation now protected black Americans and ensured equality (see Chapter 6, pages 98–100, for further legislation). By the end of the 1960s, Americans had seen the civil rights movement change from a peaceful, non-violent organisation to one which was populated by radical gun-carrying socialists who had shoot-outs with the police. The movement's outstanding figure was assassinated and the 1960s ended with nationwide riots on the death of King.

TASKS

1 What image does Source A project of the Black Panthers?

2 Study Source B. Which of these aims do you think Martin Luther King would have opposed and why?

3 Study Source C. Explain why the Black Panther movement was seen as a threat to US society.

4 How successful was the Black Panther movement? (For guidance on how to answer this type of question, see page 96.)

5 What were the most important factors in bringing about improved civil rights for black Americans between 1950 and 1963?

In your answer you may wish to discuss the following:

- the campaign for equality in education
- the campaign for equality in public transport
- the role of Martin Luther King
- the role of Malcolm X

and any other relevant factors.

(For guidance on how to answer this type of question, see pages 108–110.)

6 Working in pairs, copy the table below and complete it using the information from this chapter.

What had been achieved for black Americans by 1965?	What were the remaining issues for black Americans after 1965?

Examination guidance

This section provides guidance on how to approach tasks like those in question (c) in Unit 3. This question requires you to make a judgement about a turning point or the importance or success of a particular event, movement or individual. It is worth 8 marks.

How important was the issue of education to the civil rights movement? (8 marks)

Tips on how to answer

- This question requires you to **evaluate the importance or success** of a particular event, movement or individual.

- You must aim to **analyse and evaluate** the reasons for this importance/success.

- Descriptive answers will not score you more than half marks – **you *must* analyse**.

- You need to support your observations with **specific factual detail**.

- Remember that this question requires you to **provide a judgement**, giving specific reasons why you think this event, movement or individual was important or successful.

- You can, in certain circumstances, **disagree** and argue that the event, movement or individual was not important or successful.

Response by candidate

During the 1950s the NAACP led the fight against segregation in education. In 1954 the NAACP fought the Linda Brown case which resulted in the declaration by the Chief Justice that segregation in education was illegal and against the US constitution. However, this did not stop many schools in the South continuing with segregation and it took further action in the area of secondary education before change took place. In 1957 nine black students attempted to attend the all-white Little Rock High School but the Governor of Arkansas used the National Guardsmen to prevent them from entering. It took President Eisenhower's decision to send 1,000 paratroopers to Little Rock before the black students were allowed to attend.

These events helped the civil rights movement because they showed the unfairness of the educational system and gave weight to the campaign to bring about change. It was therefore an important battle ground for the civil rights movement and coincided with other developments at that time such as the fight to end segregation on public transport.

Comment on the candidate's performance

This is a detailed and well-structured answer. The candidate addresses the key issue throughout and provides several examples to show how education was used to challenge the segregation laws and secure civil rights. The concluding paragraph provides a judgement and some context, thereby helping to evaluate the importance of education in the fight for civil rights. The answer meets the requirements of Level Four, providing an informed and accurate analysis and evaluation of the key issue which addresses the thrust of the question.

Now you have a go

Was the fight to end segregation on public transport the most important factor in gaining civil rights for black Americans? (8 marks)

6

How much progress has been made by black Americans since the 1960s?

Source A From a speech by President Kennedy, 1963

I hope that every American will stop and examine his conscience. Today we are committed to a world-wide struggle to promote and protect the rights of all who wish to be free. And when Americans are sent to Vietnam or West Berlin we do not ask for whites only. Now the time has come for the nation to fulfil its promise ... The fires of frustration and discord are burning in every city, North and South ... We face therefore a moral crisis ... it is time to act in Congress.

TASK

Study Source A. What did President Kennedy mean by the following?
- '... every American will stop and examine his conscience'
- 'We face therefore a moral crisis ...'
- '... it is time to act in Congress'.

You have already seen in Chapter 5 that some progress had been made in the campaign for civil rights by the end of the 1960s but there was still entrenched racism in the South. Martin Luther King had put the issue of civil rights at the forefront of US domestic politics and the demonstrations of 1963 (see page 88) meant that resisting change could no longer be justified. After 1963, there were several pieces of legislation which aimed to ensure equality for black Americans.

Since the 1960s huge changes have occurred and the number of black elected officials increased quickly in the last three decades of the century. Two black politicians stood for the presidential nomination for the Democratic Party in the 1970s and 1980s and in 2008 the USA elected its first black president.

During the latter part of the twentieth century, black Americans have excelled in all fields – politics, sport, entertainment, media and literature.

This chapter addresses the following issues:

- Why was the civil rights legislation of the 1960s important?
- Why were there race riots in the 1960s?
- What has been the extent of change and progress for black Americans since the 1960s?

Examination guidance
Throughout this chapter you will be given the opportunity to practise different exam-style questions. You will also be given guidance on how to approach tasks like those used in Questions 4, 5 and 6 in Unit 3. This requires you to identify and discuss change and development over time. It is worth 12 marks, with an additional 3 marks awarded for spelling, punctuation and grammar.

Why was the civil rights legislation of the 1960s important?

▶ The Civil Rights Act of 1964

Following the assassination of President Kennedy, his successor, Lyndon Johnson, was able to push the Civil Rights Bill through the **House of Representatives** and the Senate ensuring that those southern Democrats who opposed the Bill would be counterbalanced by Republicans. Johnson had been in high-level politics since 1938 and he needed all his skills to persuade and cajole the Republicans to vote with him. He had put forward his vision of a 'Great Society' (see page 30) which would attack racial injustice and poverty. This was in the same spirit as Kennedy's 'New Frontier'.

There was deep shock within the USA following Kennedy's assassination and there were those in Congress who voted sympathetically for the Bill. Johnson was able to win some support in Congress because he was a southerner, from Texas.

The Civil Rights Act is seen by many as President Johnson's greatest achievement. However, there were many black Americans who criticised it as being insufficient and coming rather late in the day. Naturally,

there were many white Americans in the South who resented it and sought to make it fail.

▶ Voting rights

Voting rights

In 1870, by the Fifteenth Amendment, male black Americans were given the right to vote. However, some states **disenfranchised** them by such means as unfair taxation and literacy tests. The literacy tests were not a test of reading and writing – they asked difficult arithmetic and cultural questions which most people would have found impossible.

In 1962, the US government set up the Voter Education Project. The Project was staffed mainly by members of the Student Non-violent Coordinating Committee (SNCC) and they spent much time with eligible voters showing them how to register and overcome the barriers which were placed in front of them – for example, the mathematical questions which were impossible to answer. The project did result in more than 650,000 new voter registrations but many people were still refused the right to vote on dubious grounds. The SNCC workers were subject to harassment – in Georgia, several churches were bombed, workers were beaten up and some were shot. Those who did register and subsequently voted were sometimes evicted from their land, sacked from their job and refused credit.

In 1965, Martin Luther King and his colleagues decided to force the issue by embarking on another non-violent campaign. The town of Selma, Alabama, was to be the battleground as there were only 383 black American voters who had been able to register out of a possible 15,000. The sheriff of Selma, Jim Clark, had a reputation to match that of 'Bull' Connor in Birmingham (see page 87). King was hoping for a brutal reaction to his demonstrations because he knew that the press and television would again highlight the continued bigotry of the South.

There were two months of attempts to register black voters and two months of rejections. King and his followers were subjected to beatings and arrests. One

The Civil Rights Act, 1964

- Segregation in hotels, motels, restaurants, lunch counters and theatres was banned.
- The Act placed the responsibility on the federal government to bring cases to court where discrimination still occurred.
- Any business engaged in transactions with the government was monitored to ensure there was no discrimination.
- Black students were given equal rights to enter all public places and bodies which received government money, including schools.
- The Fair Employment Practices Committee, which had been set up during the Second World War (see page 72), was established on a permanent basis.
- The Act created the Equal Employment Opportunity Commission (EEOC) to implement the law.

demonstrator was murdered. It was decided to hold a march from Selma to the state capital, Birmingham, in order to present Governor Wallace with a petition asking for voting rights. Governor Wallace banned the march but King was determined to take his supporters and lobby Wallace.

The march took place on 7 March but was stopped on the Edmund Pettus Bridge where the marchers were attacked by Sheriff Clark's men and state troopers. The marchers faced tear gas, horses and clubs and were forced to return to Selma. This became known as 'Bloody Sunday' and the event forced President Johnson's hand. A second march took place two days later but King turned the marchers back – he had agreed with Johnson that he would avoid violent confrontation with Clark again.

Public opinion across the USA was firmly behind King and the civil rights movement and on 15 March President Johnson promised to put forward a bill that would enfranchise black Americans. Eventually, it was agreed that a march from Selma to Montgomery would go ahead if it was peaceful. King led more than 25,000 people on 21 March – this was the biggest event that had ever been seen in the South.

TASKS

1 Explain why some black and white Americans criticised the Civil Rights Act of 1964.

2 How important was the Civil Rights Act of 1964? (For guidance on how to answer this type of question, see page 96.)

3 Write a newspaper article praising the passing of the Civil Rights Act. Limit your headline to about six words.

4 What information does Source A provide about the civil rights march from Selma?

5 Was King justified in putting the lives of his followers at risk in the Selma marches? Explain your answer.

6 How successful were the Selma marches? (For guidance on how to answer this type of question, see page 96.)

Source A The civil rights march to the Edmund Pettus Bridge, Selma, 7 March 1965

The Voting Rights Act, 1965

The success of the Selma march created an atmosphere of optimism and, in the summer, President Johnson introduced the Voting Rights Bill which was quickly enacted by Congress. The Act:

● ended literacy tests
● ensured federal agents could monitor registration – and step in if it was felt there was discrimination. It was thought that if less than 50 per cent of all its voting-age citizens were registered then racial discrimination could be presumed.

By the end of 1965, 250,000 black Americans had registered to vote (one-third had been assisted by government monitors who checked that the law was being followed). A further 750,000 registered by the end of 1968. Furthermore, the number of elected black representatives increased rapidly after the Act.

King's policy of non-violence appeared to have worked. There was widespread support and sympathy from white Americans and there had been two key pieces of legislation which had removed discrimination and disenfranchisement.

However, other groups were emerging that opposed King's idea of non-violence. There was a feeling among some that progress was slow and that, too often, King had been ready to make deals with the white authorities (see Chapter 5, page 88).

Further civil rights reforms were introduced before President Johnson left office in 1968:

● 1967: the Supreme Court declared that state laws forbidding inter-racial marriages were unconstitutional.
● 1968: the Fair Housing Act. Discrimination in housing based on race, colour, gender, national origin, or religion was outlawed.

Source B Table showing registered voters in certain states in the USA, 1969

State	Percentage of white people registered	Percentage of black people registered
Alabama	94.6	61.3
Arkansas	81.6	77.9
Florida	94.2	67.0
Georgia	88.5	60.4
Louisiana	87.1	60.8
Mississippi	89.8	66.5
North Carolina	78.4	53.7
South Carolina	71.5	54.6
Tennessee	92.0	92.1
Texas	61.8	73.1
Virginia	78.7	58.9
USA as a whole	80.4	64.8

TASKS

7 What information does Source B provide about voters in the USA in 1969?

8 Re-read the sections on the Civil Rights Act (page 98) and the Voting Rights Act (above). Which do you think was the more important? Copy and complete the table below.

Civil Rights Act more important because ...	Voting Rights Act more important because ...

9 Had Martin Luther King's 'dream' of equal treatment for black Americans come true by the end of 1968?

Why were there race riots in the 1960s?

Source A The National Guard and police facing rioters in Detroit, 1967

Despite the civil rights laws, many young black Americans were frustrated, and those living in the ghettos felt anger at the high rates of unemployment, continuing discrimination and poverty. On 11 August 1965, this frustration exploded into a major riot involving 30,000 people in the Watts district of Los Angeles. The riot left 34 dead, 1,072 injured, 4,000 arrested and caused about $40 million of damage. There were riots across the USA's major cities in the two following summers. Many of the riots followed a similar pattern – the arrest of a black youth, a police raid, rumours of police brutality and then the explosion of the riot.

Racial violence peaked in the summer of 1967, when there were riots in 125 US cities. The two largest riots occurred in July: Newark left 26 dead and over 1,000 injured, and Detroit left more than 40 people dead, hundreds injured and 7,000 arrested. During the three summers of riots, more than 130 people were killed and damage totalled more than $700 million.

The riots of 1965–67 caused President Johnson and his advisers to look into the factors behind them. The Kerner Report (1968) stated that racism was deeply embedded in American society. It not only highlighted the economic issues faced by black Americans but also the 'systematic police bias and brutality' and recommended federal initiatives which would mean increased expenditure. The report was largely ignored.

The year of 1968 did seem to be the end of an era. The Vietnam War had begun to dominate the domestic scene and the student movement also took centre stage. However, there had been significant changes and the civil rights legislation of the 1960s had given equality and protection before the law. Yet the riots of 1965–67 and those that erupted on the death of Martin Luther King in 1968 indicated that there was still huge frustration among the black population.

TASKS

1 Study Source A. What does it show you about the riot in Detroit?

2 Describe the race riots of 1965–67 in America. (For guidance on how to answer this type of question, see pages 41–42.)

3 Why has 1968 been seen as the 'end of an era'?

What was the extent of change and progress for black Americans?

There has been tremendous change for black Americans in the latter part of the twentieth century. The election of a black American president, Barack Obama, in 2008 is testimony to the advances that have been made. Black Americans have contributed greatly to the development of all aspects of life in their country.

You have already seen in Chapter 5 that black Americans became more proud of their racial and cultural heritage in the mid-twentieth century and the phrase 'black is beautiful' was coined. Black Americans have experienced success in all walks of life since the 1960s, ranging from politics to sport, and their achievements have been recognised across the world. In most instances it was a case of being the first black American to achieve an award or position and these individuals opened the door for many more of their race.

Yet, it should be remembered that improvements in the lives of black Americans have been uneven.

▶ Politics

There has been limited success in national politics. Only 121 black Americans have been elected to both branches of the US Congress since 1880. Shirley Chisholm became the first black woman elected to Congress in 1968 and in 1972 she made a bid for the Democratic Party's presidential nomination, losing to George McGovern. Twelve years later, the Reverend Jesse Jackson made a bid for the Democratic Party's presidential nomination, but lost to Walter Mondale. Carol Moseley-Braun became the first black woman to be elected as US Senator in January 1993. However, there has been reasonable success for black Americans at local level since 1964. Many cities now have black mayors and councillors (see Source A).

Importantly, Colin Powell became the first black American to become Chairman of the Joint Chiefs of Staff in 1989 and held this crucial position during the Gulf War of 1990–91. He was the first black Secretary of State, holding the post from 2001–05.

TASKS

1 What information does Source A provide about the involvement of black Americans in politics in the years 1970–2000?

2 Write your own caption for the photograph of Obama and Jackson on page 103.

Source A Table showing black elected officials in the USA, 1970–2000

Year	Male	Female	Total	Percentage of all officials
1970	1309	160	1469	10.9
1975	2973	530	3503	15.1
1980	3936	976	4912	19.9
1985	4697	1359	6056	22.4
1990	5420	1950	7370	26.5
1995	5782	2637	8419	31.3
2000	5921	3119	9040	34.5

Barack Obama greeting Jesse Jackson at the funeral service for civil rights leader Dorothy Height, 29 April 2010

▶ Economics

Source B From an article about civil rights in a British magazine for GCSE history students

There were definite improvements in the quality of life for many of America's disadvantaged; in 1965, 19 per cent of black Americans earned the average wage, by 1967, this had risen to 27 per cent; in 1960, the average educated reading age of a black American was 10.8, by 1967 this had increased to 12.2.

By the end of the 1960s large numbers of black Americans still continued to live below the poverty line. They lived in the poorer areas of cities, went to the poorest schools and generally experienced greater deprivation than white Americans. One US university study in the 1980s showed that a middle-class black American with a PhD had less chance of living in a white neighbourhood than a Spanish-American who left school after the third grade. Many banks continued to hesitate to grant mortgages to black Americans even though they could afford expensive homes.

Source C Yearly income of black American families

Year	Income ($)	Number of families
1970	20,000 – 49,000	1.9 million
1980	20,000 – 49,000	2.3 million
1987	20,000 – 49,000	2.6 million

Source D Weekly wages of black American manual workers as a percentage of white male workers' wages

Year	1970	1980	1990	2000
Memphis	63	73	71	78
Atlanta	62	75	75	78
Washington	72	80	81	83
New York	75	76	77	78
Philadelphia	79	77	77	77
Baltimore	71	78	76	79
Chicago	75	75	74	74
Detroit	81	83	81	78
Los Angeles	74	77	81	80
San Francisco	78	79	82	80

TASKS

3 What information does Source C provide about the income of black Americans during the 1970s and 1980s?

4 Look at Sources B and D about the lives of black Americans. Explain why the quality of the lives of black Americans improved after 1960. (For guidance on how to answer this type of question, see pages 60–62.)

Education

Source E Higher educational attainment of black and white males in the United States

	Percentage of black males				Percentage of white males			
	1970	1980	1990	2000	1970	1980	1990	2000
First degree	5	9	9	10	16	23	18	20
Post-graduate degree	1	1	4	4	2	3	11	11

There was still some opposition to integration in schools even after the Civil Rights Act of 1964. Yet some cities tried to ensure integration and an ethnic mix by bussing students across racial divides. President Nixon was against bussing and in 1973 the Supreme Court banned it. There was still hardly any racial mix in some cities by 1978.

Many black Americans continue to drop out of high school and, by 2000, graduation rates and college enrolment rates were comparable to those of whites in 1975. However, the picture is not *too* bleak – between 1980 and 2007, the college enrolment rates for black Americans increased from 44 per cent to 56 per cent.

Sport

Black American athletes have always excelled at sport but in some fields they were either excluded or could only participate in segregated competitions. Since 1960, black male and female sporting heroes have emerged in all sports and have become world and Olympic champions.

In boxing, black Americans have produced some of the best heavyweights in the history of the sport. In the 1960s, Muhammad Ali emerged as world heavyweight boxing champion. He won the title three times and dominated the sport for more than twenty years. Most boxing experts view him as the greatest boxer of all time. In 1999, Ali was crowned 'Sportsman of the Century' by *Sports Illustrated* (a US sports magazine) and 'Sports Personality of the Century' by the BBC.

Similarly, US athletics has produced great black champions over the years. Carl Lewis won nine Olympic gold medals in his career, four of which were at the 1984 Los Angeles Olympics. With Michael Johnson he holds the record for the most number of medals won by any athlete. In the 1984 Olympics, black women, who accounted for only 6 per cent of the US

Muhammad Ali defending his boxing title against Sonny Liston, May 1965

population, won 75 per cent of all the track and field medals won by American women. By the time Jackie Joyner-Kersee retired from professional athletics, she had won three gold, one silver and two bronze medals in the Olympic Games.

In golf and tennis, the 'whites only' policy was the rule long after baseball, football, and basketball had integrated black and white athletes.

In tennis, Althea Gibson was the sole black female tennis star in the 1950s, and Arthur Ashe was the sole black male champion during the 1970s. Ashe was the first black American to win the US Open (1968), the

Australian Open (1970) and Wimbledon (1975). In the 2000 Olympic Games, Venus Williams won the singles gold medal and the doubles gold with her sister Serena. This was to be the beginning of a decade where the two black American women dominated world tennis.

Nowhere was the resistance to the integration of black Americans into sport more complete than in golf, where the maintenance of a system of open racism prevailed for many years. It was only in 1975 that the first black American (Lee Elder) played at the Masters tournament at Augusta. Elder then became the first black American to play for the USA in the Ryder Cup in 1979. Eldrick 'Tiger' Woods became the first black American to win the Masters golf tournament in 1997.

▶ Television

Television has produced many programmes which have created black American stars. Each decade seemed to produce more success. In the 1960s, *I Spy* was an extremely popular series starring Bill Cosby. Other shows in the 1980s and 1990s starring black Americans were *Diff'rent Strokes* with Gary Coleman and *The Fresh Prince of Bel-Air* with Will Smith. The immensely popular TV mini-series *Roots* was based on the book by Alex Haley. The programme showed the trials of a black American tracing his origins back to the early eighteenth century.

A 1999 Screen Actors Guild study showed that 16 per cent of the characters on network television were black American. This statistic is significant when compared to the fact that only 13 per cent of the American population was black at the time of the study.

Oprah Winfrey has her own television chat show but is also an actress, producer, and philanthropist. She is one of the richest people in the USA. She has become a role model for black American women.

Despite many successes in television, black Americans have found it difficult to break into the world of sports presentation. Only in the past few years have sportscasters such as Greg Gumbel and Robin Roberts moved into prestigious network positions. Other top presenters are Stuart Scott, Fred Hickman and Nick Charles.

Oprah Winfrey has used her television programme to promote literature through Oprah's Book Club. She has brought writers a far broader audience than they otherwise might have received and has influenced their increasing sales

TASKS

5 Outline the achievements of black Americans in sport and television between 1970 and 2000. (For guidance on how to answer this type of question, see pages 41–42.)

6 Suggest reasons why many black Americans have found success in boxing and athletics but so few in golf and tennis.

Literature

As in other fields, there have been great successes in literature. Toni Morrison won the Nobel Prize for literature in 1993. Writers such as Alice Walker and Maya Angelou are internationally renowned. Robert Hayden became the first black American poet laureate (1976–78) and Rita Dove was the first female poet laureate (1993–95).

Cinema

In the cinema, the last 30 years has produced many black American stars such as Eddie Murphy, Samuel L. Jackson, Morgan Freeman, Whoopi Goldberg and Angela Bassett. Denzel Washington became the second black American to win an Oscar for best actor and has played iconic roles such as Malcolm X and Steve Biko. Many of these actors have become involved in national politics, some are fundraisers for black organisations and others work on black youth projects.

One of the most influential directors in the latter part of the century has been the black American Spike Lee. Lee's movies have examined race relations, the role of media in contemporary life, urban crime and poverty.

Music

Black Americans have made enormous contributions to the world of popular music. In the 1960s, the record label Tamla Motown produced such groups as the Supremes, Martha and the Vandellas, the Four Tops, Smokey Robinson and the Miracles, the Temptations, Marvin Gaye, Stevie Wonder and the Jackson Five. From the Jackson Five there emerged Michael Jackson, who became a worldwide pop music phenomenon. His 1982 album, *Thriller*, topped the music charts all over the world and became the biggest selling album of all time.

Source F The musician Smokey Robinson on Motown's cultural impact

I recognized the bridges that we crossed, the racial problems and the barriers that we broke down with music. I recognized that because I lived it. I would come to the South in the early days of Motown and the audiences would be segregated. Then they started to get the Motown music and we would go back and the audiences were integrated and the kids were dancing together and holding hands.

Since the 1980s

Black Americans have developed their own new unique styles of music with hip hop and rap. Some politicians, journalists and religious leaders have accused rappers of creating a culture of violence and hedonism through their lyrics. However, there are also rappers whose messages include political criticism and social comment. One leading rapper is Ice T, whose first albums focused on stories of drug dealing, pimping and gang warfare, featuring an outlaw or 'gangsta' image that he carefully cultivated. For some white middle-class Americans rap music is a threatening art form, but for some black Americans, it represents a way of expressing how they live.

Source G From a speech by Pat Buchanan, candidate for the Republican presidential nomination, to a small college in Los Angeles at the time of the Rodney King riots, May 1992

But where did the mob come from? It came out of rock concerts where rap music celebrates raw lust and cop killing.

Source H From a newspaper interview with the rapper Ice T. It was published during the Rodney King riots in May 1992

I'm not saying I told you so, but rappers have been reporting from the front for years … black people look at cops as the Gestapo. People thought it might come to an end [with the Rodney King trial] and they might get some justice. That was a false hope. People saw that justice is a myth if you're black. Of course people will riot.

The riots in Los Angeles, 1992

Despite all the progress that was made in civil rights, there were riots across the USA in 1992 following the arrest of Rodney King, a black American, in Los Angeles (see page 39). During King's arrest he was assaulted by the police. A passer-by happened to have a video camera and filmed the whole incident. The police officers were eventually put on trial but were acquitted of any crime.

News of the acquittal of the police officers triggered riots across Los Angeles because black Americans perceived that there was an unfair legal system. The riots were so serious that the army, Marines and National Guard had to be used to restore order: 53 people were killed, 2,383 injured, 9,000 arrested and more than 7,000 fires were started in the city. There were damages to 3,100 businesses and it was estimated that financial losses totalled about $1 billion. Black community leaders in Los Angeles pointed out that under the presidencies of Reagan and Bush Snr in the 1980s and early 1990s there had been 60 per cent cuts in job training for black Americans and 82 per cent cuts in subsidised housing.

Some people drew the conclusion that the presidents did not want to tax Americans in order to solve the problem of black poverty. It was white Americans who paid the bulk of taxes. Not all black Americans have enjoyed prosperity and, in 1990, 50 per cent of all black children lived below the poverty line and black **infant mortality rate** was 19 per cent – higher than in some developing world countries.

TASKS

7 How successful have black Americans been in the cinema and music business since the 1970s? (For guidance on how to answer this type of question, see page 96.)

8 Study Sources G and H. Why was there a concern about rap music in America during the 1990s?

9 Copy and complete the table below. For each heading give reasons why you think it has helped to change the lives of black Americans since 1960.

Television	Literature	Sport	Cinema	Music	Individuals	Politics

10 Write a brief newspaper article about the Rodney King case.

11 What have been the most important factors in changing the lives of black Americans since 1960?

In your answer you may wish to discuss the following:

- the Civil Rights Act 1964
- the Voting Rights Act 1965
- involvement in politics
- sporting and cultural achievements
and any other relevant factors.

(For guidance on how to answer this type of question, see pages 108–111.)

Examination guidance

This section provides guidance on how to approach tasks like those used in Questions 4, 5 and 6 in Unit 3. This question requires you to identify and discuss change and development over time, in this case between 1930 and 2000. The question is worth 12 marks, together with an additional 3 marks for spelling, punctuation and grammar.

How did the lives of black Americans change between 1930 and 2000? (12 marks + 3 marks SPaG)

In your answer, you may wish to discuss the following:

- the impact of the Second World War
- the civil rights movement
- progress made by black Americans by 2000

and any other relevant factors.

(Two different sample answers to this question are given on pages 109 and 110.)

Tips on how to answer

This is a synoptic essay type question which is intended to cover the whole period you have studied. Your aim is to outline the degree of change or lack of change across the period 1930–2000. It is essential that you:

- include **information from across the whole period**, although you can be selective. For example, the Depression years; the impact of the Second World War; changes in the 1950s and 1960s; events in the 1970s and 1980s; recent developments to 2000

- **take notice of the information provided in the scaffold** and ensure that you cover those points, as well as additional information from your own knowledge of this topic

- aim for **a marriage between chronological awareness and differentiation**

- aim to show how things have changed or stayed the same, remembering that **the pace of change will vary across time** – it will be faster during some periods than others

- remember that **change did not impact upon all sections of society in the same way:** for example, not all Americans enjoyed the suburban lifestyle of the 1950s; while some black Americans became successful in the post civil rights era, not all of them did and many continued with a restricted lifestyle

- **do not dwell too long on one time period** and aim to cover as much of the period as possible

- remember the **rules of essay writing**. Your answer will require an **introduction**, several paragraphs of **discussion**, and a reasoned **conclusion**

- you will be assessed upon the quality of your written communication, with marks being awarded for spelling, punctuation and grammar.

Response by Candidate A

During the 1930s the position of black Americans was not good. They were segregated from the white Americans in almost everything they did, they were hated by the KKK and many other white activists and many were unemployed. African American children were not allowed to attend the same schools as white children, many went to schools which had no heating, their windows were smashed in and buildings were in disrepair. Things started to look up for black Americans during the Second World War when the first black American airmen, called the Tuskegee Airmen, were praised for never losing a plane. Another turning point was the civil rights movement in which the likes of Martin Luther King demonstrated using means of sit-ins, marches and bus boycotts in order for black Americans to gain more civil rights. The civil rights movement was successful in helping the lives of black Americans improve because schools were integrated, buses were de-segregated and more and more black American people were getting jobs. Lives for black Americans were improving and many black Americans were becoming famous, such as Vanessa Williams who became the first African American Miss America in 1983. More African American famous people who came into the spotlight are Michael Jackson and the Jackson Five, and actors such as Denzel Washington and Samuel L. Jackson.

The essay lacks depth and coverage of the whole period.

Limited structure to essay – no introduction or conclusion.

Comment on Candidate A's performance

This answer displays a reasonable chronological grasp but with imbalanced coverage and only some reference to the extent of change. It touches upon the situation in the 1930s, the impact of the Second World War and the work of Martin Luther King. Reference is made to the progress of black Americans in recent times but there is no attempt at differentiation. The response demonstrates sufficient understanding to edge into Level Three and could be awarded 7 marks. Spelling, punctuation and grammar are accurate with some use of specialist vocabulary, but there is no introduction or conclusion and consequently is worthy of receiving 2 rather than 3 marks.

Response by Candidate B

An informed paragraph on the lack of progress during the 1930s.

Under the constitution of the USA, all Americans are equal but a loophole in the law allowed the southern states to segregate blacks from whites on the basis that separate was equal. The Jim Crow Laws segregated black Americans in public life. The KKK was still active and the Depression in the 1930s hit black Americans hardest. The New Deal helped black Americans because they were poor, not because they were black. Some migrated north in search of a better life where there was no segregation.

Identifies the major changes of the 1950s and 1960s. There is an attempt to differentiate the degree of success.

When the USA entered the war in 1941, many black Americans enlisted in the armed forces while others worked in factories but racism continued on the fighting and home fronts. Membership of the NAACP increased. In the 1950s, the issue of education highlighted the problem. The <u>Brown v. Topeka</u> case was a victory and made segregation illegal but by the end of 1956 there were no black children attending integrated schools. Similarly, black students were admitted to Little Rock High School after the President got involved, yet by 1960 only 2,500 out of 2 million black children were attending integrated schools in the state of Arkansas. When Rosa Parks refused to give up her seat on a bus in Montgomery in 1955, the Civil Rights Movement took a dramatic turn. Martin Luther King's leadership in the boycott led to a historic victory as segregation was made illegal on buses.

Martin Luther King's programme of peaceful protest culminated in the famous 'I have a Dream' speech in front of 250,000 black and white supporters in Washington in 1963. However, some black Americans became frustrated at the slow pace of change and rejected King's passive, Christian approach and turned to the Nation of Islam, advocating violence and a separate black state within the USA. Led by Malcolm X and Stokely Carmichael many black youths turned to the Black Panthers. The Civil Rights Act of 1964 together with subsequent changes to the law ended discrimination – but did it?

Goes beyond the 1960s with clear reference to success / lack of success in the 1980s and 1990s.

Change has come about but the pace of change has been uneven for different groups of society. There have been gains and losses. In 1984 the Rev. Jesse Jackson stood for president, and throughout the 70s and 80s blacks also made steady gains in academic achievement, greatly increasing the size of the black middle class. In 1983, President Reagan set up a national holiday on 20 January as Martin Luther King Day. In the armed forces, General Colin Powell became chairman of the Joint Chiefs of Staff and played an important role in the Gulf War. On TV Bill Cosby had a massive success with the Cosby Show, which was the first programme to show a well-off middle class family. In music Michael Jackson's album 'Thriller' became the best seller of all time. However, Reagan's presidency did see the reversal in the fortunes of many black Americans. In 1990 the average wage of a black family was less than half of the average of a white family. By 1999, the average income of African American families was $33,000 compared with $55,000 for European Americans. Change has occurred for black Americans but its pace has varied and its impact has not been universal.

Differentiation upon the degree of change.

Comment on Candidate B's performance

This is a structured and well-informed account which provides an effective overview of the main developments between 1930 and 2000. There is a clear attempt to discuss the extent of change and a recognition of the varying impact of change. The last paragraph attempts a judgement which addresses the thrust of the question. Spelling, punctuation and grammar are consistently accurate with good use of specialist vocabulary. There is a structured introduction and conclusion. The answer reaches Level Four and is worthy of maximum [12] marks and 3 marks for SPaG.

How and why did US foreign policy change between 1930 and 1945?

Source A From a speech about the League of Nations made by Henry Cabot Lodge to the US Senate, August 1919

I object in the strongest possible way to having the United States agree, directly or indirectly, to be controlled by a league which may at any time be drawn in to deal with internal conflicts in other countries, no matter what those conflicts may be. It must be made perfectly clear that no American soldiers can ever be engaged in a war or ordered anywhere except by the constitutional authorities of the United States.

TASK

Study Source A. What does it tell you about the USA and the League of Nations?

During the 1920s the USA followed a foreign policy which was based on **isolationism**. The USA had no desire to become involved in any international conflicts and as a result rejected the peace treaties of 1919–20 and then refused to join the **League of Nations**.

Nevertheless, as the world political situation grew worse during the 1930s from the threat of dictatorships and military regimes, the USA continually had to reconsider its isolationist policy. The various neutrality acts of the 1930s (see page 114) highlighted US policy but despite pressure to keep out of the European conflict after 1939, the USA found itself at war against Japan after the attack on Pearl Harbor in December 1941. Within days of the attack, Germany declared war on the USA and the policy of isolation was quickly forgotten. Involvement in the Second World War led to the USA becoming the foremost power in the world.

This chapter addresses the following issues:

- Why did the USA follow a policy of isolationism?
- How did the USA become involved in the war in Europe in the years 1939–41?
- What was the USA's role in Europe and the Pacific?
- Why did the USA drop the atomic bomb?

Examination guidance
Throughout this chapter you will be given the opportunity to practise different exam-style questions. You will also be given guidance on how to approach tasks like those used in question (b) in Unit 3. This requires you to identify and explain the extent of change and/or continuity in a key issue or development through the comparison of two sources and the use of your own knowledge. It is worth 7 marks.

Why did the USA follow a policy of isolationism?

At the end of the First World War in 1918, the USA rejected the agreed peace settlement and decided not to join of the League of Nations. Some Americans said that the peace treaties would lead to future wars and that US involvement would be costly in terms of lives and money. Moreover, Europe was far away and had nothing to do with the USA. Some politicians feared loss of sovereignty if the USA joined the League and this contradicted all that the USA had fought for when it had become independent from Britain.

However, the USA did work with the League with regard to health and slavery projects. There was also close involvement when there were economic problems and in 1924 the American banker Charles Dawes chaired the committee set up by the League to settle Germany's **reparations** problems. The Dawes Plan helped restore economic prosperity to Germany.

The USA also wanted to ensure its own security and was a participant of the Washington Naval Conference in 1922 during which the five major powers of the world (Britain, France, USA, Italy and Japan) agreed on specific ratios of ships for their navies. In 1928, the USA also signed, with more than 60 other nations, the Kellogg–Briand Pact which renounced war as a means of settling international grievances.

▶ Roosevelt's foreign policy

The 'Good Neighbor Policy'

When Roosevelt became president in 1933, the majority of members of Congress were isolationists and there were some who felt that the USA should have nothing whatsoever to do with any other country because not only was the USA economically strong, but it was also far away from international hotspots.

Like previous presidents, Roosevelt had no intention of becoming involved in European affairs. He wanted the USA to follow a policy of friendship towards other countries and thought the USA could act as a 'moral force' for good in the world. The economic crisis facing the USA was his foremost task. He encouraged economic co-operation through the idea of the 'Good Neighbor Policy'.

Source A From a newspaper article written by Senator Gerald Nye, a leading isolationist, 1937

There can be no objection to any hand our government may take which strives to bring peace to the world, so long as that hand does not tie 130 million people into another death march. I very much fear that we are once again being caused to feel that the call is upon America to police a world that chooses to follow insane leaders. We reach now a condition on all fours with that prevailing just before our plunge into the European war in 1917. Will we blindly repeat that futile venture?

At the 1933 Montevideo Inter-American Conference, Uruguay, the USA and other Latin American states all agreed that no country had the right to intervene in either the internal or external affairs of another. By 1938, the Good Neighbor Policy had led to ten treaties with Latin American countries which in turn led to huge increases in trade for the USA. Roosevelt proved that he would keep his promise of the Montevideo conference in 1938 when he took no action when Mexico nationalised some US-owned oil companies.

▶ Relations with Japan

Relations with Japan were an issue for the USA throughout the 1920s and 1930s. Though there was agreement about naval limitations at the 1922 Washington Conference, relations worsened following the passing of the National Origins [Immigration] Act of 1924 which virtually ended Japanese migration to the USA. However, there was some increasing concern over the rising power of Japan.

The Japanese needed extra land and resources for their fast-growing population. In 1931, Japanese troops had invaded the Chinese province of Manchuria. President Hoover strongly disapproved of the invasion and he morally condemned it, but did not support the idea of sanctions against Japan. Six years later Japan invaded northern China and bombed Shanghai and other Chinese cities. At first, the USA simply supported the League of Nations in branding Japan as an aggressor and gave financial aid to the Chinese. Roosevelt did not begin **trade sanctions**, and merely asked Americans to boycott Japanese silk.

USS *Panay* incident

In December 1937, Japanese bombers sank the USS *Panay* and three tankers belonging to the US Standard Oil Company on the Yangtze River at Nanking. Two Americans were killed and 30 were wounded. The US government demanded an apology, compensation and a guarantee that there would not be a repeat of such an incident. The Japanese did as they were asked and paid $2 million compensation. It was only after 1940 that relations with Japan began to deteriorate seriously.

TASKS

1 Explain why the USA followed a policy of isolation after 1918.

2 In what ways did US foreign policy in the 1920s contradict the idea of isolationism?

3 What arguments are put forward in Source A to support the claim that America should remain isolationist in the late 1930s?

4 Describe Roosevelt's Good Neighbor Policy. (For guidance on how to answer this type of question, see page 144.)

5 Explain why relations between the USA and Japan became strained during the 1930s.

6 Copy and complete the table below.

Reasons for taking action against Japan during the 1930s	Reasons for not taking action against Japan during the 1930s

The USS *Panay* sinking after the Japanese air attack, 12 December 1937

▶ The neutrality acts

The widespread feeling in the USA that involvement in the First World War had been a mistake continued throughout the 1930s and was made evident when Congress passed a series of neutrality acts which were intended to keep the USA out of future wars.

1935 First Neutrality Act	The president had the power to prohibit US ships from carrying US-made munitions to countries at war (an arms embargo). He could also prevent US citizens from travelling on ships of those at war except at their own risk.
1936 Second Neutrality Act	This banned loans or credit to countries at war.
1937 Third Neutrality Act (January)	This act allowed nations involved in a war to buy goods other than munitions from the US provided they paid cash and used their own ships. It was also intended to prevent involvement in the Spanish Civil War. It forbade the export of munitions for the use of either of the opposing forces in Spain.
1937 Fourth Neutrality Act (May)	This authorised the president to list commodities other than munitions to be paid for on delivery and made travel on ships of countries at war unlawful.
1939 Fifth Neutrality Act	The president authorised **cash-and-carry** export of arms and munitions to countries at war.

However, there were problems for Roosevelt. His views began to change in the later 1930s and they differed from those of Congress and, most importantly, the majority of the American people. Roosevelt despised the spread of **totalitarianism** in Germany and Italy and by 1937 he began to see that the US might need to become involved in European affairs. For some the idea of US involvement in someone else's problems was completely detestable and for others going to war would end the reforms of the New Deal (see pages 13–15). Nevertheless, Roosevelt was able to expand the US navy and, in 1938, $1 billion was allocated for the continued development of this force. Yet, the US army had only 100,000 men and the air force about 1,600 planes. The USA was not prepared for war.

Source B From a speech by President Roosevelt, October 1937. He was speaking about the Japanese attack on China

> Without a declaration of war and without warning or justification of any kind, civilians, including vast numbers of women and children, are being ruthlessly murdered by bombs from the air ...
> If these things come to pass in other parts of the world, let no one imagine that America will escape, that America may expect mercy, that this Western Hemisphere will not be attacked ...

TASKS

7 In what ways did the neutrality acts change over the years 1935–39?

8 Study Source B. What message is Roosevelt attempting to put across?

How did the USA become involved in the war in Europe in the years 1939–41?

Source A From a speech by Charles Lindbergh, 15 September 1939, twelve days after Britain declared war on Germany. Lindbergh was a very popular figure in the USA following his solo flight across the Atlantic. He became a leading member of the isolationist America First Committee (see below)

We must not be misguided by foreign propaganda to the effect that our frontiers lie in Europe. One need only glance at a map to see where our true frontiers lie. What more could we ask than the Atlantic Ocean on the East and the Pacific on the West?

When war broke out in Europe in September 1939, President Roosevelt stated on the radio that the USA would not become involved. Ordinary Americans had differing views about the war in Europe. On the one hand, there was the Committee to Defend America (CDA), set up in 1939, which supported Roosevelt in wanting to help Britain – short of going to war. The CDA argued that the war meant that the USA was no safer than any other country. On the other hand, the America First Committee (AFC), set up in 1940, opposed anything that might risk American neutrality. The AFC felt that Britain continued to refuse to negotiate with Hitler because they wanted to convince America to enter the war on their side.

By July 1940, German successes in Europe led Roosevelt to believe that Hitler might take over French territory in the Caribbean. He organised a conference in Cuba that month and by the Act of Havana, the countries of North and South America stated that in the interests of their defence they could take over and administer any European possession in the New World which faced aggression. By this it was hoped to prevent any European colony being captured by Nazi Germany.

September 1940 was a most important month for the USA because it showed that the policy of isolationism was not as clear-cut as Americans thought. In September:

- Congress increased the budget for defence spending
- Roosevelt passed the first peacetime conscription draft, which required all men between the ages of 21 and 35 to enlist. The men who were drafted had to serve in the armed forces for one year. The peacetime draft of 1940 also meant that, if needed, the soldiers could fight for the USA or its allies
- an embargo was placed on the sale of scrap iron and steel to Japan
- the USA gave Britain 50 ageing destroyers in return for strategic naval bases in the Caribbean and Newfoundland.

Source B From an article in the *New York Times*, August 1940

Were the control of the seas by Britain lost, the Atlantic would no longer be an obstacle – rather it would become a broad highway for the conqueror moving westwards. There is no escape in isolation. We have only two choices: we surrender or we can do our part in holding the line.

TASK

1 Look at Sources A and B about attitudes to America's role in the world. Explain why American foreign policy had changed by the early 1940s. (For guidance on how to answer this type of question, see pages 126–28.)

What was Lend-Lease?

During the presidential campaign of 1940, Roosevelt made a speech in October about the USA and the war in Europe. He said:

'I have said this before, but I shall say it again and again and again. Your boys are not going to be sent into any foreign wars.'

After the presidential election campaign, it was clear that attitudes in America were changing. The defeated Republican, Wendell Wilkie, called for all Americans to support Roosevelt's policy to aid Britain against the fascists. The British sought continued help from America and in March 1941 Congress passed 'The Act Further to Promote the Defence of the United States'. It became known as the Lend-Lease agreement. This gave Roosevelt the power to 'transfer or lend' arms and other goods to any country 'whose defence was necessary to US defence'. Britain was able to defer payment for the goods which in the course of the war totalled $31.4 billion.

Source C From a radio broadcast by President Roosevelt, September 1940. Roosevelt was explaining his decision to offer Lend-Lease.

Some of our people like to believe that wars in Europe and in Asia are of no concern to us. But it is a matter of most vital concern to us that European and Asiatic war-makers should not gain control of the oceans which lead to this hemisphere. If Great Britain goes down, the Axis Powers will control the continents of Europe, Asia, Africa, Australasia, and the high seas ... It is no exaggeration to say that all of us in all the Americas would be living at the point of a gun.

Indirect involvement in the European war continued to grow in 1941 and Roosevelt was always able to say that his actions were purely for the defence of the USA:

● Hitler's invasion of the Soviet Union in June enabled Roosevelt to offer Stalin goods to the value of $1 billion via the Lend-Lease scheme.
● In July, US forces were stationed in Iceland to prevent any German takeover.

Source D A British cartoon published shortly after the publication of the Atlantic Charter, August 1941. The two men in the middle are Roosevelt and Churchill

What was the Atlantic Charter?

In August 1941, President Roosevelt and Winston Churchill met on a ship off Newfoundland and issued what became known as the Atlantic Charter. The meeting lasted four days and the two leaders established a set of goals for the post-war world:

● free trade in the world
● freedom of the seas
● freedom for people to choose their own government
● an end to the use of armed force
● the final destruction of Nazi tyranny.

By the end of September, fifteen other countries had signed the Charter and the idea was put forward of an international organisation to protect the security of all countries. (This was the origin of the United Nations.)

During the summer of 1941, US assistance to Britain grew. Destroyers escorted convoys of British merchant ships as far as Iceland and, in addition, some British ships were repaired in US shipyards. In September, an American destroyer was attacked by a German submarine after which Roosevelt ordered the US navy to shoot on sight at German or Italian warships. The following month the American destroyer *Reuben James* was sunk off Iceland with the loss of 115 lives. Congress revised the neutrality acts to allow US merchant ships to arm and also carry munitions directly to Britain. The change in attitude was very obvious. Isolation was at an end. By the end of November 1941, few Americans supported the idea of isolationism. Indeed, some 15,000 American had enlisted either in the Canadian or British armed forces.

Source E From President Roosevelt's Address to the Nation, 11 September 1941

We have sought no shooting war with Hitler. We do not seek it now ... But when you see a rattlesnake poised to strike, you do not wait until he has struck before you crush it. These Nazi submarines and raiders are the rattlesnakes of the Atlantic.

Source F From *The Second World War*, Winston Churchill, 1949. Here he is talking about Roosevelt and the Atlantic Charter

Had he (Roosevelt) not acted when he did, in the way he did ... a hideous fate might well have overwhelmed mankind and made its whole future for centuries sink into shame and ruin. It may well be that he not only anticipated history but altered its course, and altered it in a manner which has saved freedom and earned the gratitude of the human race for generations to come.

TASKS

2 Make a list of reasons to explain why the Committee to Defend America (CDA) would support the actions of Roosevelt and Congress and why the America First Committee (AFC) would criticise them.

3 Study Source C. Explain why President Roosevelt introduced the Lend-Lease scheme.

4 Describe the Atlantic Charter. (For guidance on how to answer this type of question, see page 144.)

5 What is the message of the cartoon shown in Source D?

6 Suggest reasons why so many Americans had enlisted in the British armed forces by the end of 1941.

7 Study Sources E and F. Explain why Roosevelt was prepared to take the USA into another war.

8 How successful was Roosevelt in keeping the USA isolated in the 1930s? (For guidance on how to answer this type of question, see page 96.)

Deteriorating relations with Japan, 1939–41

US relations with Japan in the 1930s were not friendly and after 1939 they deteriorated rapidly. In July 1940 there was a change of government in Japan and the new, militaristic cabinet announced the 'Greater East Asia Co-prosperity Sphere'. This was nothing more than the creation of a Japanese empire to provide living space for its growing population. Japan then became a member of the Three Power Pact of September 1940 with Germany and Italy. Japan hoped this would warn America against any future military action against Japanese expansion.

America's reaction was to try to bring the Japanese under control by economic pressure. In July 1940, certain US exports to Japan were forbidden. US trading agreements with Japanese companies were cancelled and the sale of planes, chemicals and iron was stopped. Relations came to a head in July 1941 when Japan invaded the French colonies in Indo-China. The Americans responded by cutting off all supplies of oil to Japan. As Japan imported almost 90 per cent of its oil from the USA, the ban was a crippling blow and the Japanese complained that their economy would collapse. The Americans insisted they would only lift the ban if the Japanese held peace talks with the Chinese.

When General Tojo became Japanese premier on 18 October 1941 the Japanese mood hardened. Desperate to find a new source of oil, the Japanese planned to attack the oil-rich British and Dutch colonies in South-East Asia. They knew that they were not strong enough to fight the Americans and the British simultaneously. Their plan therefore was to wipe out the US Pacific Fleet at Pearl Harbor in Hawaii, then attack the British.

Despite mounting tension, the Americans and Japanese continued to negotiate throughout November and December. The Japanese government was happy to continue talks to gain time to prepare for their surprise attack on Pearl Harbor.

Source G Adapted from a school textbook by B. Williams, *Modern Japan*, 1973

Japan needed something like the Greater East Asia Co-Prosperity Sphere, where its markets would be under its direct control ... the Japanese aggressive spirit had been fostered by military fanatics for their own ends. Since 1931, the military had been slowly edging themselves into a controlling position in the Japanese government. In 1941, they sought to maintain their own political power whilst gaining glory for Japan by the conquest of an empire.

Source H Speech by a member of the Japanese government to leading politicians and military leaders, 5 November 1941

In the first few months of the war it is very likely that we would achieve total victory. I am convinced that we should take advantage of this opportunity. We shall use the high morale of the Japanese people and their determination to overcome the crisis facing our country, even at the risk of losing our lives. It would be better to attack now than to sit and wait while the enemy puts more and more pressure upon us.

TASKS

9 What reasons are given in Source G to explain why Japan began to expand its empire between 1931 and 1941?

10 Explain why relations between the USA and Japan deteriorated in the period 1939–41.

11 How important was the need for oil in determining Japanese foreign policy during this period? (For guidance on how to answer this type of question, see page 96.)

Source I A US battleship blown up by Japanese planes at Pearl Harbor, 7 December 1941

The attack on Pearl Harbor

At dawn on Sunday 7 December 1941, the Japanese attacked the US naval fleet at Pearl Harbor in Hawaii. The attack was daring because it involved the Japanese force sailing more than 3,000 miles before launching its strike. US intelligence discovered the Japanese force's movements and decoded its messages but failed to warn Pearl Harbor in time. Three hundred and sixty torpedo planes and bombers, launched from Japanese carriers 400 kilometres away, attacked the US fleet. The attack resulted in 2,345 US servicemen killed, 1,240 injured, 57 civilians killed and 35 wounded.

Other damage was:

- 4 battleships sunk, 4 battleships damaged
- 2 destroyers sunk, 1 damaged
- 3 cruisers damaged
- 1 other ship sunk, 3 damaged
- 188 aircraft destroyed
- 155 aircraft damaged

Effects of the attack

In the space of two hours, the US Pacific Fleet was crippled, but in fact the attack was not as damaging as it might have been. By chance, the fleet's four aircraft carriers were not in port that day. In addition the Japanese made no attempt to destroy the huge oil storage tanks which supplied the US navy with its fuel. The immediate result was to bring the US into the war as, on 8 December, Britain and the USA declared war on Japan. Germany and Italy, as allies of Japan, then declared war on the USA.

TASKS

12 Study Source H. What reasons does the Japanese government give for launching the attack against the USA?

13 Describe the Japanese attack on Pearl Harbor in December 1941. (For guidance on how to answer this type of question, see page 144.)

14 Make a copy of the table below and complete it to show the achievements and limitations of the attack on Pearl Harbor.

Successes	Limitations

What was the USA's role in Europe and the Pacific?

▶ The war in Europe

As soon as the USA became involved in the Second World War, Roosevelt and Churchill agreed that the priority in the war was the defeat of Germany. The first US offensive was in North Africa in November 1942. By May 1943, the Germans had been defeated in North Africa and more than 250,000 German troops surrendered to the Allied forces whose Supreme Commander was US General Dwight Eisenhower. Following this victory, US and British forces invaded Sicily (July 1943) and then the Italian mainland (September 1943).

In December 1943, Roosevelt, Stalin (the leader of the Soviet Union) and Churchill met together for the first time. The 'Big Three' now agreed that the **second front** would be opened in May or June of 1944. The Soviet Union agreed to declare war on Japan as soon as Germany was defeated. After the conference, General Eisenhower was made Supreme Commander of the Allied Expeditionary Forces. By the time he took over this post, initial plans for the invasion of Normandy had been drawn up under the codename of 'Operation Overlord'.

D-Day

Hundreds of thousands of US soldiers came over to Britain. Training, feeding and keeping the troops occupied created huge logistical problems. More than a year of training was undertaken by some of the troops and many were killed during manoeuvres. The US also sent over huge quantities of military materials in preparation for Operation Overlord. Key items were landing craft (vessels to take soldiers and vehicles to the beaches) and also gliders. The gliders were to be used to land thousands of troops behind enemy lines before the assaults on Normandy's beaches took place. As Operation Overlord developed, the actual day of the invasion became known as D-Day.

D-Day began on the night of 5–6 June 1944 when paratroopers and soldiers in gliders landed in Normandy. The US landed 15,500 airborne troops and the British sent 7,900 men behind enemy lines using nearly 1,000 gliders. Almost 7,000 naval vessels assembled in the English Channel off Normandy and the first landings at the designated beaches (Utah and Omaha were the US beaches) were made at 6.30a.m. on 6 June. By the

Source A US soldiers shown just after they left a Coast Guard landing craft, headed for the Normandy beaches, 6 June 1944 (D-Day)

end of the day, the Allies had landed 156,000 troops with supporting mechanised vehicles. The US landed 23,250 men on Utah beach and 34,250 on Omaha beach, in addition to the 15,500 airborne troops. There were 2,499 American D-Day fatalities. By the end of July 1944, 1 million American, British, Canadian, French and Polish troops and hundreds of thousands of vehicles and supporting material had been landed in Normandy.

German defeat

The Allies liberated Paris in August 1944 and pushed on toward Germany. Hitler made his last stand in what became known as the Battle of the Bulge during December 1944 and January 1945. During the battle, 19,000 Americans were killed and there were 60,000 wounded, captured or missing. Germany could not match the Allies in men and supplies. Germany, trapped in a vice with the Soviet Union in the east and the US, British and other Allied forces in the west, surrendered on 8 May 1945.

TASKS

1 Outline the main events of the D-Day landings in June 1944. (For guidance on how to answer this type of question, see page 144.)

2 How successful were the D-Day landings? (For guidance on how to answer this type of question, see page 96.)

▶ The war in the Pacific

By the end of 1942, the Japanese Imperial Army had captured Burma, Malaya, the Philippines, the Dutch East Indies, parts of New Guinea and many islands in the Western Pacific (see map below). Japanese victories in the early months of the war in the Pacific had secured the country three-quarters of the world's natural rubber reserves, two-thirds of the tin, and vital supplies of oil.

Japan now sought to protect its economic gains by reinforcing its perimeter to the south, capturing Port Moresby in New Guinea and cutting off Australia. US intelligence had decoded Japanese messages and knew that an invasion force would pass through the Coral Sea. A task force of aircraft carriers and battleships was assembled to intercept and attack the Japanese convoys. This was the first naval battle in which the opposing sides never sighted one another, but relied on scout aircraft to direct attacks against one another's warships from the air. During the battle from 4–8 May 1942, both sides suffered heavy damage but the Japanese lost two aircraft carriers to America's one. Furthermore, the Japanese failed to capture the rest of New Guinea, from which they could have attacked Australia. It was their first setback. Just one month later came an even more serious defeat.

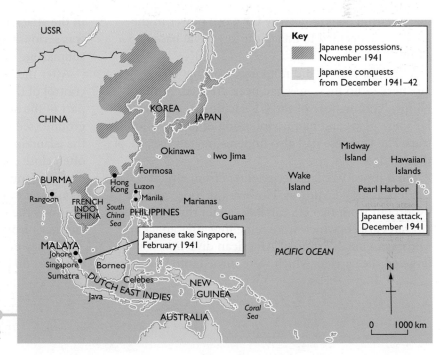

Map showing Japanese gains to 1942

▶ The Battle of Midway

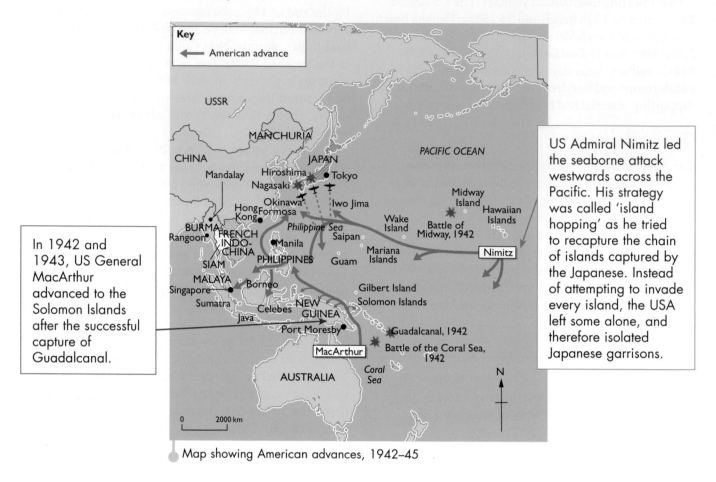

Key

← American advance

USSR

MANCHURIA

CHINA

JAPAN

Mandalay

Hiroshima • Tokyo
Nagasaki

Okinawa
Hong Iwo Jima
Formosa
Kong

BURMA
Rangoon
FRENCH
INDO-
CHINA

Manila

SIAM

MALAYA

Singapore

Sumatra

Java

Borneo

Celebes

NEW
GUINEA

Port Moresby

Philippine Sea

Saipan

PHILIPPINES

Mariana
Islands

Guam

Gilbert Island

Solomon Islands

Wake
Island

PACIFIC OCEAN

Midway
Island

Battle of
Midway, 1942

Hawaiian
Islands

Nimitz

Guadalcanal, 1942

Battle of the Coral Sea,
1942

MacArthur

*Coral
Sea*

AUSTRALIA

N

0   2000 km

In 1942 and 1943, US General MacArthur advanced to the Solomon Islands after the successful capture of Guadalcanal.

US Admiral Nimitz led the seaborne attack westwards across the Pacific. His strategy was called 'island hopping' as he tried to recapture the chain of islands captured by the Japanese. Instead of attempting to invade every island, the USA left some alone, and therefore isolated Japanese garrisons.

Map showing American advances, 1942–45

The Japanese naval commander, Admiral Yamamoto, had a daring plan to destroy US naval power in the Pacific. He decided to attack the key naval base of Midway Island.

What Yamamoto did not know was that coded Japanese radio messages had been cracked. Admiral Nimitz, commander of the US Pacific Fleet, knew the Japanese plans and had no intention of falling into their trap. The Japanese had also underestimated the size of the US fleet.

On 4 June 1942 Japanese fighters from aircraft carriers attacked Midway. However, surprise attacks by aircraft from two US carriers caught three Japanese aircraft carriers which were refuelling after attacking Midway. A small group of American dive-bombers targeted the carriers which were turned into burning wrecks. A fourth Japanese carrier escaped and joined in the attack on the US carrier, *Yorktown*, which was seriously damaged and later sunk by a Japanese submarine.

After the Battle of Midway neither side had gained control of the South Pacific. The island of Guadalcanal, part of the Solomon Islands, became the key battle ground (see map above). Both sides landed troops on the island in August 1942. This was followed by bitter often close combat fighting over the next five months until, in January 1943, the Japanese abandoned the island and evacuated their remaining 10,000 troops. This was the first successful US land battle and marked another turning point in the conflict in the Pacific.

The key events of the war in the Pacific are shown in the chart on page 123.

Timeline of US progress in the Pacific 1943–45

Date	Key event
1943 November	US troops captured the island of Tarawa in the Gilbert Islands. Out of a Japanese garrison of 4,836, only 17 surrendered.
December	US troops captured the Solomon Islands after a four-month struggle.
1944 Jan–Feb	US troops captured the Marshall Islands
June–July	US capture of Saipan. This gave the USA an airbase within bombing distance of Japan itself.
July	US invasion of Guam in the Marianas Islands. Took three weeks to capture.
August	The Battle of the Philippine Sea. A Japanese strike force of nine aircraft carriers to stop US invasion of islands. The Japanese were defeated with three carriers sunk and three damaged.
October	The greatest naval battle in history: the Battle of Leyte Gulf. Japanese attempt to prevent loss of Philippines. Japanese lose 27 major warships to 6 American warships. At this stage, the Japanese began to send kamikaze pilots against the US fleet. Kamikaze means 'Divine Wind' and pilots would deliberately crash their planes into an American battleship. To commit suicide in this way was regarded as an honourable thing. Before the end of the war kamikaze pilots had sunk 34 US ships and damaged 288 more.
1945 February	US had control of Philippines including the capital, Manila. The capture of Manila cost 1,100 US lives and 16,000 Japanese.
February–March	US troops landed on Iwo Jima which had Japanese airfields. The island was captured by the US with the loss of 4,000 US marines and 20,000 Japanese. The casualty rate reached 75 per cent in two US Marine divisions.
March	US air raid on Tokyo caused a firestorm and 80,000 Japanese were killed.
March–August	US bombing campaign using captured Japanese airfields and new B29 Superfortress bombers. The US air force destroyed a quarter of all Japanese houses in firebomb attacks. Millions abandoned the cities to seek food and shelter in the countryside, leaving factories without enough workers and reducing industrial output.
April–June	US troops invaded the island of Okinawa. It took nearly three months of bitter fighting to capture the island with even greater losses on both sides. 100,000 Japanese troops and 12,000 US troops died.

TASKS

3 Why was the Battle of the Coral Sea important for the USA?

4 Why were the battles of Midway and Guadalcanal turning points in the war in the Pacific? (For guidance on how to answer this type of question, see pages 75–76.)

5 Look at the timeline in the table above. Explain the importance of the following in the US advance of 1943–45:

- the Battle of Leyte Gulf
- Iwo Jima
- Okinawa
- kamikaze pilots.

Why did the USA drop the atomic bomb?

By the summer of 1945, almost all Japanese conquests in the Pacific had been recaptured and Japanese forces were retreating in South-East Asia. However, there was still the prospect of an invasion of Japan itself. In Japan the leadership was divided between the 'war group', who wanted to fight to the bitter end, and a 'peace group' led by Prime Minister Suzuki, who wanted to negotiate an end to the war. The government made secret approaches to the Soviet Union to act as a go-between with the USA.

The new US president, Harry Truman, decided to use the atomic bomb as a means of bringing the war to an end as soon as possible. On 6 and 9 August 1945, atomic bombs were dropped on the Japanese cities of Hiroshima and Nagasaki. Within a week the Japanese government had surrendered.

The bombs devastated the two cities. In Hiroshima, at the very centre of the explosion the heat was so great that anything caught in it turned from a solid to a gas. Further out, people were burnt alive. The explosion created a wind of 800 kilometres an hour that crushed many people. However, in many ways the worst damage was caused by radiation. It caused flesh to dissolve and hang down in strips. In Hiroshima, 80,000 people were killed, rising to 138,000 as a result of radiation sickness. In Nagasaki, 40,000 were killed, rising to over 48,000.

Source A From *Memoirs of Harry S. Truman*, 1955

In all it had been estimated that it would require until late fall of 1946 to bring Japan to her knees. All of us realised that the fighting would be fierce and the losses heavy. General Marshall told me that it might cost half a million lives to force the enemy's surrender on his home ground ... I regarded the bomb as a military weapon and never had any doubt that it should be used. In deciding to use this bomb I wanted to make sure that it would be used in a manner prescribed by the laws of war. That meant I wanted it dropped on a military target.

Hiroshima after the dropping of the atomic bomb

Source B From an interview with a US soldier shortly after the end of the Second World War

The Japanese just would not surrender. At Guadalcanal, we surrounded the Japanese in the valleys. They were tough fighters. We cut off the remains of a Japanese regiment. After we had surrounded them we used loud-speakers to try to get them to surrender. But they kept fighting. We had to go in the valleys and kill them. They would not surrender.

Five days after the bombing of Nagasaki, the Japanese government agreed to unconditional surrender. On 27 August, US forces began occupying Japan. One week later, the Japanese prime minister and military leaders signed the formal surrender on board the USS *Missouri* in Tokyo Bay.

▶ Reasons for US victory in the Pacific

The USA was able to produce more aircraft, aircraft carriers and weapons than Japan. In addition, it had a huge workforce, vast natural resources and importantly its industrial centres never came under attack. Japanese production was badly affected by US air raids. Often four out of five workers were missing from work after air-raids. Absenteeism reduced the output of Japanese industry. Steel output, which was 7.8 million tonnes in 1944, fell to 1 million tonnes in 1945. Aircraft production fell by one-third. Oil stocks, which were 43 million barrels at the start of the year, fell to just 4 million by March 1945.

The US gained command of the sea and air after the battles of Coral Sea, Midway, and Leyte Gulf. This was essential for successful operations in the Pacific Islands. Following the capture of Iwo Jima and Okinawa, the USA could use the airfields to bomb Japan at will in 1945. US submarines sank more than 75 per cent of Japan's merchant ships whilst US bombing destroyed Japanese homes and factories. In 1945 many people in Japan were starving and industrial production collapsed. From March to September 1945, 275 kilometres² of Japan's cities were destroyed by incendiary bombs. In all, a quarter of houses in Japan were destroyed. Twenty-two million people – a quarter of the population – were made homeless.

The USA had tried to avoid involvement in world affairs after 1919 but gradually found itself helping Britain against Germany and Italy after 1939. The attack on Pearl Harbor ensured that involvement in the war was certain. By the end of the war in 1945, the USA was the greatest industrial power in the world. Moreover, the possession of the atomic bomb meant that it had the military power to destroy any enemy. The policy of isolationism was no longer an option after Hiroshima and Nagasaki.

TASKS

1 Study Source A. What reasons does President Truman give for using the atomic bomb?

2 Describe the events which led to the dropping of the atomic bombs on Japan. (For guidance on how to answer this type of question, see page 144.)

3 Explain why America was successful in the war in the war in the Pacific.

4 How far did the USA's role in world affairs change in the years 1930–45?

You may wish to discuss the following in your answer:

- the policy of isolation
- the Neutrality Acts
- the war in Europe 1939–41
- Pearl Harbor

and any other relevant factors.

(For guidance on how to answer this type of question, see pages 108–110.)

Examination guidance

This section provides guidance on how to approach tasks like those used in question (b) in Unit 3. It requires you to **identify and explain the extent of change and/or continuity** in a key issue or development through the comparison of two sources and the use of your own knowledge. It is worth 7 marks.

Look at Sources A and B about American foreign policy during the 1930s and 1940s.

Source A An American politician speaking in 1935

> There will be no opposition to any action which our government takes to bring about world peace as long as it does not commit 130 million American people to another world war. I fear we are again being expected to police the world and sort out Europe's problems. We do not want to get involved in Europe.

Source B President Truman announcing the Truman Doctrine to Congress in March 1947

Explain why American foreign policy had changed by the late 1940s.
[In your answer, you should use the information in the sources and your own knowledge to show the extent of change and the reasons for this.]

(There are two sample answers to this question on pages 127 and 128.)

Tips on how to answer

This question asks you to identify change or lack of change (continuity) and to use your own knowledge to help describe and explain this change or continuity, placing each source into context. To do this you must:

- **describe** what is in each source, making use of the caption written immediately above each source

- **refer directly to each source**, for example 'Source A says … This contrasts with Source B which shows …'

- attempt to **cross-reference**, pointing out what is the same or different in each source

- remember to include **specific factual detail** from your own knowledge to help place each source in its historical context

- remember that if you only use your own knowledge and **do not specifically refer to the sources you cannot advance beyond half marks**

- ensure that you have described and explained both sources, **displayed a sharp focus on the key issue of change or continuity**, and supported this with your own knowledge of this topic.

Response by Candidate A

In the 1930s America was isolationist and did not want to get involved in the affairs of other countries. American foreign policy had changed by the late 1940s for a number of reasons. After Japan bombed Pearl Harbor America was forced to declare war and joined with Britain to fight Japan, Germany and Italy. America became more active in world affairs and when the war ended she ended up being the leader of the free world against the growing threat of communism. This marked a major change in American foreign policy from not being involved to being actively involved.

Good own knowledge but there is no direct mention of either source.

Comment on Candidate A's performance

The candidate may have used the two sources as a guide but the response contains no direct reference to either of them and this therefore confines the answer to the low Level Two band. There is good support from the candidate's own knowledge, noting the change from isolationism to active involvement, identifying the Second World War as the reason for this change of policy. However, the lack of direct reference to the sources means this response will score just under half marks.

Response by Candidate B

Throughout the 1920s and 1930s America had been determined to keep to its policy of isolationism. This is shown in <u>Source A</u> by a politician who is stating in 1935 how America will not be involved in the affairs of other countries, especially in Europe. However, complete isolation was almost impossible to achieve as America was constantly trading goods with other countries and because she had grown into such a powerful economic country.

American foreign policy was forced to change drastically after the Japanese bombed the US naval base at Pearl Harbor in Hawaii in December 1941. America was forced to abandon its isolationist policy and enter the Second World War. Once the war ended President Truman was worried by the spread of communism in eastern Europe and relations with the USSR became strained. He felt that America had a responsibility to help prevent the spread of communism and in <u>Source B</u> he is seen announcing the Truman Doctrine to Congress. This was a policy of containment, meant to offer countries help in their efforts to fight off communism.

<u>Sources A and B</u> show complete opposites in American foreign policy. <u>Source A</u> shows the traditional policy of isolationism which was broken by the actions of Japan. After the war America was determined to play a more active part in world affairs and <u>Source B</u> shows the announcement of America's role as 'leader of the free world'. This was the exact opposite to its previous policy of isolationism.

Good attempt to place Source A in its historical context.

Spells out the reason for the change in policy.

Demonstrates good own knowledge to help explain the context of Source B.

Good cross-referencing of sources and a clear explanation of change.

Comment on Candidate B's performance

The candidate has produced an informed response which names both sources, describes and explains the message of each source, and places these events into their historical context. The concluding paragraph cross-references the sources and spells out the fundamental change in US foreign policy. This is a detailed and well structured response which matches the requirements of top Level Three, being worthy of receiving maximum [7] marks.

8 How and why was the USA involved in the Cold War?

Source A Joseph Stalin speaking in 1945 about his allies Churchill, the British Prime Minister, and Roosevelt, the US President

Perhaps you think that, because we are allies of the English, we have forgotten who they are and who Churchill is. They find nothing sweeter than to trick their allies. And Churchill? Churchill is the kind who, if you don't watch him, will slip a kopek out of your pocket. And Roosevelt? Roosevelt is not like that. He dips his hand only for bigger coins.

TASK

Read Source A. Do you get the impression that Stalin trusted his allies?

In 1945 the leaders of the USA, Britain and the **USSR** met at two peace conferences, Yalta and Potsdam, to decide the future of Germany and Eastern Europe. By the end of the second conference at Potsdam, the USA and USSR had become rivals in what became known as the Cold War.

The USA adopted a policy of **containment** to stop the spread of **communism** in Europe and then the wider world. This led to a series of crises between the two **superpowers**, more especially the Berlin Blockade of 1948–49 and the Cuban Missile Crisis of 1962. In addition, the USA became involved in the conflict in Vietnam in order to prevent a communist takeover of the country. This conflict brought much opposition within the USA, especially from the student movement, and led to the eventual defeat and withdrawal of American troops.

This chapter addresses the following issues:

- Why did the USA become involved in the Cold War?
- What was the US policy of containment?
- How did the USA try to contain the spread of communism in Europe?
- What were the key features of the Cuban Missile Crisis?
- What were the key features of US involvement in Vietnam?

Examination guidance
Throughout this chapter you will be given the opportunity to practise different exam-style questions. You will also be given guidance on how to approach tasks like those used in question (a) in Unit 3. This is the describe/outline question which requires you to provide specific knowledge of an historical event. It is worth 5 marks.

Why did the USA become involved in the Cold War?

Source B The Big Three – Churchill, Roosevelt and Stalin (left to right) – at the Yalta conference in February 1945. Here they discussed what to do with Germany and Europe once victory was achieved. It was to be their last meeting

During the Second World War, out of necessity, the USA and USSR worked together in order to defeat their common enemy, Hitler and Nazi Germany. However, once Hitler's regime was defeated, in May 1945, relations between the two superpowers began to deteriorate.

In the years after 1945 the USA and the Soviet Union became involved in a cold war which lasted for over 40 years. A hot war is a conflict in which actual fighting takes place. A cold war is a war waged against an enemy by every means short of actually fighting. The USA became involved for several reasons.

▶ Fear of communism

The USA, who believed in **capitalism**, feared the spread of communism. This fear originated with the Bolshevik (communist) takeover of Russia in 1917, especially as the Bolsheviks believed in world revolution to spread communism. It was evident in the Red Scare and McCarthyism of the late 1940s and 1950s (see pages 26–29).

▶ Soviet expansion in Eastern Europe

Having freed much of Eastern Europe from the Nazis, the **Red Army** remained in occupation in this area and the Soviet Union established communist governments that were closely controlled from Moscow. These became known as Soviet satellite states and included Poland, Romania, Bulgaria, Czechoslovakia and Hungary. Truman was convinced that Stalin wanted to expand into Western Europe.

▶ Attitude of Truman

In April 1945 Harry Truman became President of the USA. Truman distrusted Stalin and was convinced that the Soviet Union intended to take over the whole of Europe. He was determined to stand up to the Soviet leader. On 16 July 1945, the Americans successfully tested an atomic bomb at a desert site in the USA. At the start of the Potsdam Conference, Truman informed Stalin about this. The Soviet leader was furious that he had not been consulted beforehand.

Source C George Kennan was a US official in Moscow. In 1946 he wrote a long telegram to President Truman warning him about Soviet expansion

It is clear that the United States cannot expect in the foreseeable future to be close to Soviet regime. It must continue to regard the Soviet Union as a rival, not a partner, in the political arena. It must continue to expect that Soviet policies will reflect no abstract love of peace and stability, no real faith in the possibility of a permanent happy coexistence of the communist and capitalist worlds. Rather, Soviet policies will be a cautious, persistent pressure toward the disruption and weakening of all rival influence and rival power.

▶ The Potsdam Conference, July 1945

The Potsdam Conference was the second peace conference of 1945, the first being Yalta in January. Truman and Stalin had several disagreements. Twenty million Russians had died during the war and Stalin wanted massive compensation that would have totally and permanently crippled Germany. Truman refused. He saw a revived Germany as a possible barrier to future Soviet expansion. Truman wanted free elections in the countries of Eastern Europe occupied by Soviet troops. Stalin refused to submit to US pressure, believing it was unwelcome interference. Truman was furious and began a 'get tough' policy against the Soviet Union.

At the Potsdam Conference, it was agreed:

- to divide Germany and Berlin as previously agreed. Each of the four zones of Germany and four sectors of Berlin was occupied and administered by one of the Allies
- to demilitarise Germany
- to re-establish democracy in Germany including free elections, a free press and freedom of speech
- that Germany had to pay reparations to the Allies in equipment and materials. Most of this would go to the Soviet Union, which had suffered most. The Soviet Union would be given a quarter of the industrial goods made in the western zones in return for food and coal from the Soviet zone
- to ban the Nazi Party. Nazis were removed from important positions and leading Nazis were put on trial for war crimes at Nuremberg in 1946
- to participate fully in the United Nations organisation
- that Poland's frontier was to be moved westwards to the rivers Oder and Neisse.

Source D Clement Attlee, the British prime minister, recalling the Potsdam Conference in 1960

The Russians had shown themselves even more difficult than anyone expected. After Potsdam, one couldn't be very hopeful any longer. It was quite obvious they were going to be troublesome. The war had left them holding positions far into Europe, much too far. I had no doubt they intended to use them.

TASKS

1 What information does Source C provide about the attitude of the USA to Soviet expansion into Eastern Europe?

2 Look at Sources B and D about relations between the USA and the Soviet Union. Explain why relations between the USA and the Soviet Union changed after 1945. (For guidance on how to answer this type of question, see pages 126–28.)

What was the US policy of containment?

In March 1946 Winston Churchill made a speech at Fulton, Missouri, USA which showed how divided Europe had become within less than a year of the end of the Second World War. In this very famous speech he suggested that 'From Stettin in the Baltic to Trieste in the Adriatic, an **iron curtain** has descended across the continent of Europe'.

▶ The Truman Doctrine of containment

In 1947 Britain, who had been giving financial aid to Greece and Turkey since 1944, told the USA they could no longer afford to give this aid. The USA stepped in with the necessary financial aid fearing that these two countries would come under Soviet influence. Truman announced US support in an important speech in March 1947. The speech marked a turning point in US foreign policy. He was committing the USA to a policy of containment that became known as the Truman Doctrine.

Source A The Truman Doctrine, 12 March 1947

I believe that it must be the policy of the United States to support peoples who resist being enslaved by armed minorities or by outside pressure. I believe that we must help free peoples to work out their own destiny in their own way.

▶ The Marshall Plan

Truman backed up his policy of containment with economic aid to Europe. This was known as the Marshall Plan. He believed that communism generally won support in countries where there were economic problems, unemployment and poverty. Many European countries had suffered badly as a result of the Second World War and were struggling to deal with the damage caused. There were shortages of nearly everything, which led countries to implement rationing. If the USA

Source B Berliners using money from the Marshall Plan to help rebuild buildings destroyed during the Second World War

could help these countries to recover economically and provide employment and reasonable prosperity, then there would be no need to turn to communism.

The plan, officially called the European Recovery Plan but nicknamed the Marshall Plan, was announced by the US Secretary of State, General George Marshall, in June 1947. This aid would take the form of cash, machinery, food and technological assistance. In return, these countries would agree to buy US goods and allow US companies to invest capital in their industries.

US machinery helped European factories to recover from the effects of the Second World War. US advisers helped to rebuild transport systems. Europe became more firmly divided between East and West. Stalin was initially involved but withdrew the Soviet Union from discussions because he did not trust the USA and did not want to show how weak the Soviet Union really was economically. He prevented Eastern European countries, such as Czechoslovakia and Poland, from being involved. By 1953 the USA had provided $17 billion in Marshall Aid.

▶ Domino theory

Containment was based on the **Domino Theory**, the belief that if one country fell to communism this would trigger the fall of its neighbouring countries. The theory was later applied to Asia.

TASKS

1 Describe the Truman Doctrine. (For guidance on how to answer this type of question, see page 144.)

2 Study Source B. What does it show you about the Marshall Plan?

3 Was the period 1945–47 a turning point in US foreign policy? (For guidance on how to answer this type of question, see pages 75–76.)

4 What information does Source C provide about the Domino Theory?

Source C The Domino Theory

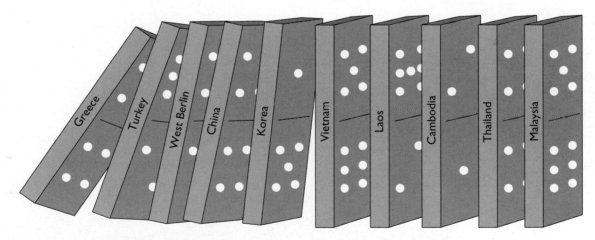

How did the USA try to contain the spread of communism in Europe?

Truman put his policy of containment into practice with the Berlin crisis of 1948–49 and the setting up of the North Atlantic Treaty Organisation (**NATO**) in 1949.

▶ The Berlin crisis of 1948–49

In 1948 Stalin blockaded all routes by land and rail into West Berlin. This sparked the first major crisis of the Cold War and worsened relations between the superpowers even further.

Map showing the division of Germany and Berlin

During the peace conferences of 1945 at Yalta (February) and Potsdam (July), the Allies had agreed to divide both Germany and Berlin into four zones of occupation (see map, page 134). Berlin was in the heart of Soviet-controlled East Germany and the western Allies were allowed access to their sectors by road, rail, canal and air.

The western Allies forged ahead by encouraging the economic recovery of their zones, especially in providing a much-needed currency. The western zones received large quantities of Marshall Aid (pages 132–133). In addition they set up free elections to establish democracy. This was in sharp contrast with

Source A A British cartoon of July 1948. The man holding the gun is Stalin and the storks represent the planes carrying supplies

THE BIRD WATCHER

Soviet policies. Stalin feared a strong, democratic and reunited Germany on the borders of the Soviet Union. He feared that a 'western' currency and democratic ideas would spread to the Soviet zone and undermine control of East Berlin. When, in 1948, the Allies announced plans to create a West German state and a new currency, Stalin accused the West of interfering in the Soviet zone. On 24 June 1948, he cut off road, rail and canal traffic to Berlin from the western zone of Germany in an attempt to starve the Allies out of West Berlin.

Truman was determined to stand up to the Soviet Union and show that he was serious about containment (see page 132). He saw Berlin as a test case. If the western Allies gave in to Stalin on this issue, the western zones of Germany might be next. Truman wanted Berlin to be a symbol of freedom behind the Iron Curtain. The only way into Berlin was by air. So the Allies decided to airlift supplies from their bases in West Germany. Would the Soviet Union shoot down these planes? There were anxious moments as the first planes flew over Berlin but no shots were fired.

The airlift began on 28 June 1948 and lasted for ten months. The British codenamed it 'Operation Plainfare'. It was the start of the biggest airlift in history. Soon planes were flying day and night along the **air corridors**. The airlift continued into the spring and reached its peak on 16–17 April 1949 when 1398 flights landed nearly 13,000 tons of supplies in 24 hours. During the airlift West Berliners were supplied with everything from food and clothing to oil and building materials, although there were still great shortages in the city and many decided to leave. During this period there were a total of 275,000 flights with an average of 4000 tonnes of supplies each day.

On 12 May 1949 Stalin called off the **blockade**. He had failed to starve the Allies out of Berlin. That evening Berliners put on evening dress and danced in the streets. The crisis greatly increased East–West rivalry, confirmed the divisions of Germany and Berlin and led to the creation of the North Atlantic Treaty Organisation or NATO. Truman saw the outcome of the crisis as a great victory. West Berlin had survived and stood up to the Soviet Union. His policy of containment had worked.

TASKS

1 You are an adviser to the western powers and have been asked to weigh up the options facing them to deal with the blockade. Which option would you advise on?

- What are the advantages and disadvantages of each option? Use the following grid to help you:

Options	Advantages	Disadvantages
Drive through the blockade		
Withdraw from Berlin		
Supply Berlin by air		

- Write a memo to the western powers giving your recommended action.
- Give reasons for your choice.

2 What is the message of Source A on page 135?

3 Explain why the Allies decided to airlift supplies into Berlin in 1948.

4 Working in pairs, put together contrasting newspaper headlines announcing the end of the airlift (one from a Soviet perspective and one from a US perspective).

▶ NATO

The Berlin crisis had confirmed Truman's commitment to containment in Europe and highlighted the Soviet threat to Western Europe. The Western European states were aware that, even joined together, they were no match for the Soviet Union and needed the formal support of the USA. In April 1949 the North Atlantic Treaty Organisation (NATO) was signed. Although a defensive alliance, its main purpose was to prevent Soviet expansion.

The countries agreed that an armed attack against one or more of them in Europe or North America would be considered an attack against them all. Stalin saw NATO as an 'aggressive alliance' aimed against the Soviet Union. Within six years, in 1955, the Soviet Union had set up its own rival organisation known as the Warsaw Pact. It was a military alliance of eight nations headed by the Soviet Union and was designed to counter the threat of NATO. Members were to support each other if attacked. A joint command structure was set up under the Soviet Supreme Commander. The creation of these two powerful and rival military power blocks fuelled the tension of the Cold War. In early 1960 Berlin again became a major flashpoint in Cold War relations.

The Berlin crisis, 1961

In August 1961, Khrushchev, the leader of the USSR, ordered the construction of a wall to separate East Berlin from West Berlin. From January 1961 the number of refugees leaving East Berlin had increased to 20,000 a month. This had to be stopped. Moreover, Khrushchev thought he could bully the new, inexperienced president of the USA, John F. Kennedy. From 5p.m. on 27 October to 11a.m. on 28 October, US and Soviet tanks, fully armed, faced each other in a tense stand-off. Then, after eighteen hours, the US tanks pulled back. Kennedy had been forced to back down but was furious with the USSR.

TASK

5 Describe how relations between the USA and the USSR changed in the years 1947–49. (For guidance on how to answer this type of question, see page 144.)

What were the key features of the Cuban Missile Crisis?

The Cuban Missile Crisis, which took place over a few days in October 1962, brought the superpowers to the brink of nuclear war. The crisis showed how the Cold War had spread outside the confines of Europe into the wider world.

Source A A map showing the Soviet Union's military build-up on Cuba and the range of the nuclear missiles

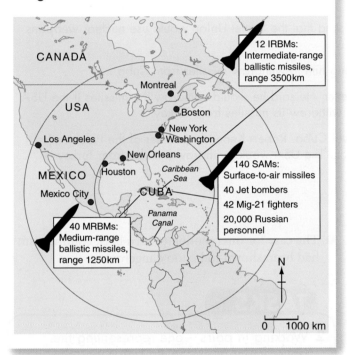

since 1934. Cuba had become very much a playground for American businessmen. However, Cuba became a thorn in the side of the USA in 1959, when a revolution had brought Fidel Castro to power. Castro had ejected all US businesses and investment. In retaliation, the USA refused to buy Cuba's biggest export – sugar. The Soviet Union offered to buy Cuban sugar. The Soviet leader Khrushchev was keen to extend Soviet influence in the Caribbean and wanted to outmanoeuvre John F Kennedy, the inexperienced American president.

In April 1961 Kennedy sanctioned an invasion of Cuba by exiles who had left Cuba in 1959. The Bay of Pigs invasion was a disastrous failure due to poor planning and lack of support in Cuba, where Castro was popular. It was a humiliation for the USA; it further strengthened Castro's position in Cuba and drew Cuba even closer to the Soviet Union. At the end of 1961, Castro announced his conversion to communism.

Khrushchev now saw the opportunity to further extend Soviet influence in Cuba. He was concerned by US missile bases in Italy and Turkey and wanted to establish Soviet bases in Cuba to redress the balance. In September 1962, Soviet technicians began to install ballistic missiles on Cuba. On 14 October an American U-2 spy plane took photographs of Cuba which showed that Soviet intermediate-range missile launch sites were being constructed. These could hit almost all US cities and posed a serious threat to the country's security.

▶ Causes

The USA had long played an important part in Cuban affairs, propping up the military dictatorship of Batista

TASK

1 Explain why there was a crisis over Cuba in October 1962.

▶ Events

The crisis lasted over thirteen days in October 1962.

16 October	Kennedy was told that Khrushchev intended to build missile sites on Cuba.
18–19 October	Kennedy held talks with his closest advisers. The 'Hawks' wanted an aggressive policy whilst the 'Doves' favoured a peaceful solution.
20 October	Kennedy decided to impose a naval blockade around Cuba to prevent Soviet missiles reaching Cuba. US forces searched any ship suspected of carrying arms or missiles.
21 October	Kennedy made a broadcast to the American people, informing them of the potential threat and what he intended to do.
23 October	Khrushchev sent a letter to Kennedy insisting that Soviet ships would force their way through the blockade.
24 October	Khrushchev issued a statement insisting that the Soviet Union would use nuclear weapons in the event of a war.
25 October	Kennedy wrote to Khrushchev asking him to withdraw missiles from Cuba.
26 October	Khrushchev replied to Kennedy's letter. He said he would withdraw the missiles if the USA promised not to invade Cuba and withdrew its missiles from Turkey.
27 October	A US spy plane was shot down over Cuba. Robert Kennedy (brother of the President) agreed a deal with the Soviet Union. The USA would withdraw missiles from Turkey as long as the deal was kept secret.
28 October	Khrushchev accepted the deal.

▶ Results

The Cuban crisis had several important results.

- Kennedy seemed to have won the war of words and the perception was that Khrushchev had backed down, especially as the deal over Turkey was not disclosed at the time.
- The superpowers had played a game of **brinksmanship**. This was typical of the Cold War and means pushing a situation to the verge of war, in order to encourage or threaten your opponent to back down.
- The superpowers had almost gone to war – a war that would have destroyed much of the world. There was a relief that the crisis was over and there was a great reduction in tension. To ensure that the two leaders did not have to communicate by letter in the case of a crisis, a hotline telephone link was established between the White House in Washington DC and the Kremlin in Moscow.
- Further improvements came when the Partial Test Ban Treaty was signed in August 1963 whereby both the USA and the USSR agreed to stop testing nuclear weapons in the atmosphere.
- The case for intervention to turn back communism had been shown to be too dangerous.

TASKS

2 Working in pairs – one representing the government of the Soviet Union and the other the government of the USA – prepare a speech which clearly supports your actions during the crisis.

3 What were the effects of the Cuban Missile Crisis on each of the following?

- Superpower relations
- The world
- Cuba
- The Soviet Union
- The USA

4 Was the Cuban Missile Crisis a turning point in Cold War relations? (For guidance on how to answer this type of question, see pages 75–76.)

What were the key features of US involvement in Vietnam?

Under President Johnson the USA became directly involved in the war in Vietnam. This involvement was to have major effects on US foreign and domestic policy.

▶ Reasons for US involvement

Vietnam had been a French colony but the defeat of the French in 1954 resulted in far greater US involvement. This was part of their policy of containment in order to stop the spread of communism. The fundamental reason was the Domino Theory (see page 133). The USA was convinced that if Vietnam fell to communism it would be followed by its neighbouring states, especially Laos and Cambodia. US involvement increased in the years 1954–64.

(see page 133)

TASKS

1 Make a copy of the table below showing possible reasons for US involvement in Vietnam in the 1950s and 1960s. Give each reason a rating of 1–5 for their importance (from 1 = unimportant to 5 = decisive.) Give a brief explanation for each decision.

Reasons	Ratings
Contain communism	
Defend democracy	
Extend US influence	

2 Explain why the USA became more involved in Vietnam in the years 1954–64.

Date	Reason	US policy
1954	The Geneva Agreement	This followed the defeat of the French at Dien Bien Phu by the **Vietminh**. Vietnam would be divided temporarily along the 17th parallel into North and South Vietnam. North Vietnam would be led by Ho Chi Minh (communist) and the South would be led by Ngo Dinh Diem (non-communist). The USA prevented early elections for a new government in July 1956, realising that the communists would win.
1959	**Vietcong** terror campaign	Ho Chi Minh issued orders to the Vietminh (who became known as the Vietcong) to begin a terror campaign against the South.
1963	Overthrow of Diem	In November 1963 Diem, who was a corrupt and unpopular ruler, was overthrown and replaced by a series of short-lived and weak governments. The Vietcong became more popular in the South.
1963	Failure of 'Strategic Hamlet Policy'	Under Kennedy, the USA tried to reduce communist influence through this policy. It involved moving peasants into fortified villages, guarded by troops. It did not stop the communists and was very unpopular with the peasants.
1964	Gulf of Tonkin incident	President Johnson wanted more direct military involvement in Vietnam but needed an excuse. On 2 August 1964 the US destroyer *Maddox* was fired on by North Vietnamese patrol boats in the Gulf of Tonkin. Johnson was able to use these attacks to persuade Congress to support greater US involvement.

US methods of warfare in Vietnam

The methods used by the USA changed during the course of the 1960s.

'Operation Rolling Thunder'

This was the US bombing campaign of North Vietnam that lasted three and half years, from 1965–68, in the hope of destroying Vietcong supply routes to the South. It encouraged even greater support for the war from North Vietnam and did not stop the supplies to the Vietcong from the North.

Chemical warfare

Chemical weapons such as **defoliants** were used to destroy the jungle cover for the Vietcong.

- One such weapon was known as 'Agent Orange', a highly toxic weedkiller used to destroy the jungle. The Americans used 82 million litres of Agent Orange to spray thousands of kilometres of jungle.
- Napalm was another chemical weapon widely used by the USA. It was a type of bomb that exploded and showered the surrounding victims with a burning petroleum jelly. Napalm sticks to the skin and burns at 800 degrees Celsius. In other words, it burned through the skin to the bone.

'Search and destroy'

The US commander in Vietnam, Westmoreland, established secure and heavily defended US bases in the south of the country near the coasts. From here, US and South Vietnamese (ARVN) forces launched 'search and destroy' tactics using helicopters. They would descend on a village suspected of assisting the Vietcong forces and destroy it. The troops called these attacks 'Zippo' raids after the name of the lighters they used to set fire to the thatched houses of the villages.

- These raids would usually kill a handful of Vietcong guerrilla fighters, but inexperienced US troops often walked into traps.
- Inadequate information often meant that innocent villages were destroyed.
- Civilian casualties were often very high with most having little or no connection with the Vietcong.

- This, in turn, made the USA and ARVN very unpopular with many South Vietnamese peasants who were then more likely to support the Vietcong.

Source A An account from Doug Ramsey, a US civilian who was working for the Agency for International Development (AID) in Vietnam. He describes what happened to one village

The rubble of the hamlet was still smoking, and it was obvious that these people had returned only a short time before to discover what had happened to their homes. Children were whimpering. Women were poking through the smouldering debris of the houses trying to save cooking utensils and other small possessions that might have escaped the flames. The soldiers had even burned all of the rice that had not been buried or hidden elsewhere. A middle-aged farmer in the group asked Ramsey what agency he worked for. 'AID', Ramsey replied. 'AID', the farmer cried. 'Look about you', he said whilst pointing at the charred ruins of the village. 'Here is your American AID'! The farmer spat on the ground and walked away.

TASKS

3 Describe the use of chemical weapons by American forces fighting in Vietnam. (For guidance on how to answer this type of question, see page 144.)

4 Study Source B on page 141. What does it show you about 'search and destroy' methods?

5 How successful were the 'search and destroy' methods used by American forces in the war in Vietnam? You may wish to use Sources A and B on pages 140–41 for information to help you answer this question.

Source B A photograph showing US soldiers destroying a village suspected of supporting the Vietcong

▶ Reasons for US defeat

The USA were eventually defeated in Vietnam due to the strengths of the communists and their own weaknesses.

The strengths of the communists	The weaknesses of the USA
Fighting for a cause • The North Vietnamese and Vietcong were fighting for a cause – communism and the reunification of Vietnam. • They refused to surrender even after US bomb attacks. • They were prepared to accept heavy casualties. *Effective guerrilla tactics* • The Vietcong fought a 'low-tech' war using very successful **guerrilla** tactics which, for the most part, avoided pitched battles and reduced the effectiveness of the 'high-tech' methods and superior weaponry of the USA. • These methods were ideally suited to the jungle terrain of South Vietnam. *Support from the Soviet Union and China* • Both of these countries supported the reunification of Vietnam under the communist North. They supplied the North and Vietcong with rockets, tanks and fighter planes. *Support from the South Vietnamese* Many in the South supported the North and the Vietcong: • Some believed in communism and reunification • Others were alienated by US tactics and brutality. Their support, in turn, made the Vietcong guerrilla tactics far more effective. *The tunnels* The communist forces dug deep tunnels and used them as air-raid shelters. They were also a safe haven for the guerrilla fighters. They often acted as death traps for US and ARVN forces.	*The US troops* • Many were too young and inexperienced and unable to cope with guerrilla warfare. Most did not understand why they were fighting in Vietnam. • This, in turn, led to a fall in morale with some resorting to drug-taking and brutal behaviour such as that seen in the My Lai massacre where, in March 1968, US troops murdered 347 men, women and children. *Opposition at home (see page 52)* This undermined the war effort and was due to: • a failure to achieve a quick victory • many casualties, with a total of 58,000 deaths • televised pictures showing the horrors of war such as the use of napalm. *Failure of US tactics* • The US army failed to develop an effective response to Vietcong guerrilla tactics. • US tactics, especially 'search and destroy' and chemical warfare, encouraged even greater peasant support for the Vietcong in the countryside. *The Tet Offensive* On 31 January 1968, the Vietcong launched a massive attack on over 100 cities and towns in South Vietnam during the New Year, or Tet holiday. This proved an important turning point in the conflict: • It showed that the Vietcong could strike at the heart of the American-held territory. Even the US Embassy in Saigon was captured. • It brought a further loss of US military morale. • To the US public, the war seemed unwinnable and it fuelled further criticism of US involvement.

▶ The US withdrawal

Source C A Vietnamese poster of 1968 showing the guerrilla warfare used by the Vietcong

Source D A US soldier remembers his first battle. From C. Culpin, *Making History*, 1996

We were in the middle of dense jungle with insects everywhere. Oh God, I was so scared! My stomach was churning. I suspected I was going to vomit and also have a bowel movement at the same time. I remember thinking I would rather throw up because it would not show. The last thing I wanted to do was fight.

By 1969, more than 36,000 members of the US military had been killed in the war. In May of that year, President Nixon, who had been elected the previous year on a promise of withdrawing US troops from Vietnam, unveiled his plan to end US involvement, known as **Vietnamisation**. The idea was that the South Vietnamese soldiers would be trained and equipped to take the place of US troops as they were gradually withdrawn. The strategy did not work because the South Vietnamese troops were no match for the communist forces.

Peace talks to end the war had begun as early as 1968 but made no real progress until Nixon's visit to China in 1972 (see page 148) after which the Chinese encouraged more co-operation from the government of North Vietnam. On 23 January 1973, a ceasefire was signed in Paris, followed four days later by a formal peace treaty in which the USA promised to fully withdraw all its troops and the Vietcong was allowed to hold on to all captured areas of South Vietnam. Within two years, the communists had defeated the South Vietnamese armed forces and reunited Vietnam. The US had failed in its attempts to stop the spread of communism in South-East Asia. Cambodia and Laos also fell to communism, proving the Domino Theory partially true.

The effects of the war

- The USA spent around $30 billion each year on the war. This did much to undermine Johnson's spending on the Great Society (see page 30).
- The war made President Johnson very unpopular and heavily influenced his decision not to seek re-election as president in 1968.
- The American policy of containment had failed. The war had shown that even the USA's vast military strength could not stop the spread of communism. Not only did the USA fail to stop Vietnam becoming communist, but the heavy bombing of Vietnam's neighbours, Laos and Cambodia, encouraged support for communism in both countries. Indeed, by 1975, Laos and Cambodia had communist governments. Far from slowing down the domino effect, US policies had advanced the process in South-East Asia.

- The Vietnam War was also a propaganda disaster for the USA which did much to lessen its influence in world affairs. It was shown to be propping up a corrupt government in South Vietnam. Moreover, the atrocities committed by American soldiers and the use of chemical weapons damaged the reputation of the USA and its defence of capitalism.
- The inability to win the war pushed Nixon into considering different diplomatic strategies that affected the Cold War. His decision to visit China to establish closer relations, and also to develop **détente** (see pages 146–147) with the Soviet Union, were attempts to drive a wedge between the two main supporters of North Vietnam.
- From the war emerged the Nixon Doctrine which stated that the USA expected its allies to take care of their own military defence. The Vietnam War was the first war that the USA had lost and there was an unwillingness to become involved in future conflicts.

TASKS

6 Produce a mind map showing the reasons for US defeat in Vietnam. Draw lines to show links between the reasons, giving a brief explanation for the link along each line.

7 Explain why US forces were defeated in the conflict in Vietnam. You may wish to use Sources C and D for information to help you answer this question.

8 What have been the most important factors in bringing about change in the foreign policy of the USA in the years 1945–74? In your answer you may wish to discuss the following:

- the Truman Doctrine and Marshall Plan
- the Berlin crisis, 1948–49
- the Cuban Missile Crisis, 1962
- the war in Vietnam

and any other relevant factors.

(For guidance on how to answer this type of question, see pages 108–110.)

Examination guidance

This section provides guidance on how to approach tasks like those used in question (a) in Unit 3. It is a describe/outline question which requires you to provide specific knowledge of an historical event. It is worth 5 marks.

Outline the main methods of warfare used by American forces in the Vietnam War. (5 marks)

Tips on how to answer

- The question is asking you to **describe** or **outline** a key historical event.

- Make sure you only include information which is **directly relevant**.

- Jot down your initial thoughts, **making a brief list** of the points you intend to mention.

- After you have finished your list try to put the points into **chronological order** by numbering them.

- It is a good idea to start your answer **using the words of the question**. For example, 'The main methods of warfare used by American forces in Vietnam were …'.

- Try to include **specific factual details** such as dates, events, the names of key people, important policies. The more informed your description the higher the mark you will receive.

- Aim to write a **good sized paragraph**, covering **at least three key features/points**.

Response by candidate

At the time of the Vietnam War America was one of the world's two leading superpowers and had access to the most powerful and technologically advanced weapons. She used these to fight the Vietcong. Between 1965-68 America followed 'Operation Rolling Thunder' which involved the intense bombing of VC supply routes in North Vietnam. America also used chemical weapons such as Agent Orange which was a type of weed killer sprayed from planes over the jungle in order to locate VC bases. Napalm bombs filled with petroleum jelly were dropped on suspected VC hideouts, and this burned intensely when exposed to the air. American forces also carried out 'Search and Destroy' missions, using helicopters to drop US troops into villages to search for VC members and to set fire to the buildings hiding the enemy. Despite these weapons America still found it very difficult to deal with the guerrilla tactics used by the VC.

Comment on candidate's performance

The candidate has provided a detailed and accurate outline of the key methods of warfare used by American forces in the Vietnam War. At least three methods of warfare are identified and described – heavy bombing, use of chemical weapons and the use of helicopters to search for and destroy VC hideouts. There is sufficient depth of understanding and supportive factual detail to warrant the awarding of maximum [5] marks, placing the answer at the top of Level Three.

Now you have a go

Describe the key events of the Cuban Missile Crisis. (5 marks)

What role has the USA played in the search for world peace since 1970?

Source A A cartoon of 1982 showing President Reagan on the left and Brezhnev, leader of the Soviet Union, on the right

During the 1970s the USA supported a policy of improved relations with the Soviet Union, known as détente. The key features of this policy were the Helsinki Agreements and Nixon's visit to China. This warming of friendship came to an abrupt end with the Soviet invasion of Afghanistan in 1979 which plunged the world into a second phase of the Cold War. However, during the late 1980s co-operation between the USA and USSR improved once again due to the close working relationship of Reagan and Gorbachev and was followed by the end of the Cold War. The last twenty years of the twentieth century, on the other hand, saw the USA become increasingly concerned about developments in the Middle East, more especially Iran and Iraq.

This chapter addresses the following issues:

- What were the key features of détente?
- How did Nixon change relations with China?
- What was the significance of the Soviet invasion of Afghanistan?
- How did the Cold War change under Reagan and Gorbachev?
- Why did the Cold War end?
- What were the key features of US involvement in Iran, Iraq and the Gulf War?

TASK

Study Source A. What does it show you about relations between the USA and the USSR in the early 1980s?

Examination guidance
Throughout this chapter you will be given the opportunity to practise different exam-style questions. At the end of this chapter you will be given an overview of Questions 2–6 of the Unit 3 examination paper.

What were the key features of détente?

The improvement in relations between the USA and the USSR in the years after the Cuban Missile Crisis (see pages 137–139) became known as détente – a French word that means a reduction in tension.

▶ Reasons for détente

This relaxation in relations was due to several reasons.

● The threat of a nuclear war during the Cuban Missile Crisis had had a sobering effect on all concerned. The hotline between the White House and the Kremlin improved the speed of communications and the Test Ban Treaty (see page 138) showed a willingness to look at the issue of developing nuclear missiles.

● Both the USA and the USSR were keen on arms limitation talks as a means of reducing their ever-increasing defence spending.

● The USA involvement in Vietnam had not gone well and, by 1968, the USA was seeking to end the war. After Nixon became president it was hoped that if the USA improved trade and technology links and made an offer of arms reduction, then Leonid Brezhnev, the Soviet leader, might persuade his North Vietnamese ally to negotiate an end to the war. The idea of offering concessions was called '**linkage**' by Nixon's advisers. Nixon visited Moscow in 1972 and made it clear that he did not see Vietnam as an obstacle to détente.

● Nixon had visited China three months earlier (see page 148) and Brezhnev did not want to see a Chinese–US alliance develop. The Soviet leader was keen to gain access to US technology and further grain sales.

● The Soviet invasion of Czechoslovakia in 1968 gave rise to the Brezhnev Doctrine. This declared that all member countries had to remain part of the Warsaw Pact. In other words, the USSR would put down any attempt to suppress communist control. This alarmed the USA and showed the need for dialogue between the two superpowers.

▶ Détente in action

The SALT agreements

SALT stands for Strategic Arms Limitation Treaty. There were two such treaties.

	SALT I	SALT II
Terms	Early in Nixon's presidency, a decision was made to talk about nuclear weapons. Talks held in Helsinki and Vienna over a period of almost three years produced SALT I, the first Strategic Arms Limitation Treaty, which imposed limits on the nuclear capability of the USSR and the USA. ● The two superpowers agreed that there would be no further production of strategic ballistic missiles (short-range, lightweight missiles). ● Both powers agreed that submarines carrying nuclear weapons would only be introduced when existing stocks of intercontinental ballistic missiles (ICBM) became obsolete.	Final agreements for SALT II were reached in June 1979. The terms were: ● a limit of 2400 strategic nuclear delivery vehicles for each side ● a 1320 limit on multiple independently targetable reentry vehicle (MIRV) systems for each side ● a ban on the construction of new land-based intercontinental ballistic missiles (ICBM) launchers ● the agreement would last until 1985.
Significance	SALT I was significant because it was the first agreement between the superpowers that successfully limited the number of nuclear weapons they held.	The US Senate refused to ratify the SALT II agreements following the Soviet invasion of Afghanistan, December 1979.

Source A Brezhnev (left) and Nixon (right) at the signing of SALT I in 1972

The Helsinki Agreements, 1975

In July 1974 Nixon visited Moscow. After the meeting the two leaders agreed to develop broad, mutually beneficial co-operation in commercial, economic, scientific, technical and cultural fields. The aim was to promote increased understanding and confidence between the peoples of both countries. The Helsinki Agreements of 1975 were a product of this. The USA and the USSR, along with 33 other nations, made declarations about three distinct international issues (called 'baskets' by the signatories).

The Apollo–Soyuz mission, 1975

This was a joint space mission in which an American Apollo spacecraft and a Soviet Soyuz spacecraft docked high above Earth. This marked the beginning of superpower co-operation in space.

SECURITY

Recognition of Europe's frontiers. Soviet Union accepted the existence of West Germany.

HUMAN RIGHTS

Each signatory agreed to respect human rights and basic freedoms such as thought, speech, religion and freedom from unfair arrest.

CO-OPERATION

There was a call for closer economic, scientific and cultural links – these would lead to even closer political agreement.

The three issues (or 'baskets') discussed under the Helsinki Agreements, 1975

TASKS

1 Make a copy of the Venn diagram below showing the reasons for détente. Complete each section of the diagram.

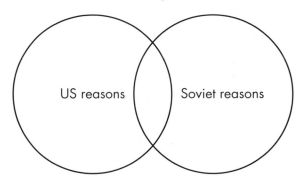

US reasons   Soviet reasons

2 Describe the Helsinki Agreements. (For guidance on how to answer this type of question, see page 144.)

3 What information does Source A provide about relations between the USA and the Soviet Union in the early 1970s?

How did Nixon change relations with China?

In October 1970, in an interview with *Time* magazine, Nixon said: 'If there is anything I want to do before I die, it is to go to China.' In the early 1970s, he was to achieve this wish.

▶ Reasons

There were several reasons for improved relations between the USA and China.

- Relations between China and the USSR had worsened in the later 1960s, especially after the Chinese denounced the Soviet invasion of Czechoslovakia in 1968. Nixon saw an opportunity to exploit this split between the two leading communist nations.
- Nixon also hoped that closer relations with China might help to end the war in Vietnam, as the Chinese were close allies of the North Vietnamese (see page 141). This was another example of his policy of linkage.
- In April 1971, the USA lifted its 21-year-old **trade embargo** with China.

▶ 'Ping-pong diplomacy'

'Ping-pong diplomacy' began at the World Table Tennis Championship held in Japan on 6 April 1971, when the Chinese ping-pong team formally invited the US team to play in their country on an all-expenses paid trip. When American player Glenn Cowan missed his team's bus after practice, he was offered a ride by Chinese player,

Zhuang Zedong. This friendly display of good will was well publicised and later that day the American team was formally invited to China. They were among the first group of US citizens permitted to visit China since 1949.

On 14 April 1971, the US government lifted a trade embargo with China that had lasted over twenty years. Talks began to facilitate a meeting between top government officials and, eventually, a meeting between China's leader Mao Zedong and President Richard Nixon. In February 1972, Nixon would become the first American president to visit China. The meeting did help to normalise relations between the two countries and reduce tensions over Vietnam.

This 'ping-pong diplomacy' was important because it led to the restoration of Sino-US relations which had been cut for more than two decades. This triggered off a series of other events, including the restoration of China's legitimate rights in the **United Nations** by an overwhelming majority vote in October 1971 and the establishment of diplomatic relations between China and other countries. Moreover, the lifting of the embargo with China meant that trade between the two countries could be restored. However, the economic benefits of this were slow as it would take decades for American products to penetrate the vast Chinese market.

TASK

Explain why the USA wanted improved relations with China.

The US table tennis team pose for a portrait with their guides in front of a pagoda at the Summer Palace near Beijing, China in April 1971

What was the significance of the Soviet invasion of Afghanistan?

Between 25 December 1979 and 1 January 1980, more than 50,000 Soviet troops were sent to Afghanistan to restore order and protect the People's Democratic Party of Afghanistan (PDPA) from the Muslim guerrilla movement known as the *mujahideen*. The invasion was to profoundly change the Cold War and relations between the superpowers.

▶ The reaction of President Carter

President Carter adopted a firm approach with the Soviet Union over the invasion. This was because he was already under pressure in November 1979 following the seizure of US embassy staff as hostages in Iran (see pages 156–158). He had failed to solve that problem by the end of the year, and some in the USA were accusing him of being a weak leader. In addition, he believed it would improve relations with China, who also opposed the invasion. He therefore adopted a firm approach with the Soviet Union over the invasion.

- The Carter Doctrine stated that the USA would use military force if necessary to defend its national interests in the Persian Gulf region. It also promised US military aid to all the countries bordering Afghanistan.
- The tough line was continued when Carter asked the Senate to delay passing the SALT II treaty (see page 146).
- The USA cancelled all shipments of grain to the Soviet Union and US companies were forbidden to sell high-tech goods there, such as computers and oil drilling equipment.
- Carter pressured the United States Olympic Committee to boycott the 1980 Moscow Olympic Games. Sixty-one other countries followed Carter's example.

Source A From Carter's State of the Union speech (an annual address by the President to the country) on 23 January 1980

Let our position be absolutely clear: an attempt by any outside force to gain control of the Persian Gulf region will be regarded as an assault on the vital interests of the USA, and such an assault will be repelled by any means necessary, including military force.

Source B Map showing the geographical importance of Afghanistan

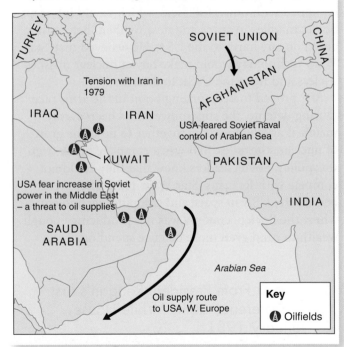

Source C From a newspaper article in the Chinese newspaper, *Beijing People's Daily*, 1 January 1980. It was discussing the Soviet invasion of Afghanistan

The invasion is a stepping-stone for a southward thrust towards Pakistan and India. There will be no peace in Southern Asia with Soviet soldiers in strategic Afghanistan.

Reagan and the 'Second Cold War'

Ronald Reagan, who defeated Carter in the 1980 presidential election, believed in taking a far tougher line with the Soviet Union than Carter. He made it clear that he had no interest in détente and was prepared to confront the USSR whenever possible. In a speech to the British House of Commons on 8 June 1982, Reagan called the USSR 'an evil empire'. He was determined to win the Cold War and believed that the USSR could be forced to disarm by his new initiative: SDI (Strategic Defence Initiative).

SDI

The Strategic Defence Initiative, which became known as 'Star Wars', took the nuclear arms race to a new level. It proposed a 'nuclear umbrella', which would stop Soviet nuclear bombs from reaching American soil. Reagan's plan was to launch an army of satellites equipped with powerful lasers, which would intercept Soviet missiles in space and destroy them before they could do any harm to the USA. He believed that 'Star Wars' technology would make Soviet nuclear missiles useless and force the USSR to disarm.

SDI proved to be a turning point in the arms race. During détente, the superpowers had been evenly matched and had worked together to limit the growth of nuclear stockpiles. SDI was a complete break from this policy. Soviet leaders knew that they could not compete with Reagan's 'Star Wars' plan. They were behind the USA in space and computer technology whilst the Soviet economy was not producing enough wealth to fund even more defence spending.

Source D From President Reagan's first press conference at the White House, 31 January 1981

So far, détente has been a one way street which the Soviet Union has used to pursue its own aims. I know of no leader of the Soviet Union who has not more than once repeated in communist congresses that their goal must be the promotion of world revolution and a one-world communist state.

Source E Two comments about the Cold War and communism that President Reagan made during his first presidency

Here's my strategy on the Cold War: We win, they lose.

Communism works only in heaven, where they don't need it, and in hell, where they've already got it.

By the early 1980s relations between the two superpowers had deteriorated to such an extent that this period is often described as the beginning of the second Cold War.

TASKS

1 Explain why Presidents Carter and Reagan adopted a hardline policy towards the USSR. You may wish to use Sources A (page 149) and D (left) for information.

2 Study Source C. What can you learn about the reaction of China to the Soviet invasion?

3 Describe the Strategic Defence Initiative. (For guidance on how to answer this type of question, see page 144.)

4 Look at Source A (page 149) and Source E (above) about relations between the USA and the USSR. Explain why relations between the USA and the USSR changed between 1972 and 1984. (For guidance on how to answer this type of question, see pages 126–28.)

How did the Cold War change under Reagan and Gorbachev?

The relationship between the USA and the USSR changed again in the mid-1980s because of Gorbachev's new policies and his relationship with Reagan.

▶ Gorbachev's new policies

Mikhail Gorbachev was the last leader of the USSR, serving as General Secretary from 1985 until its collapse in 1991. He oversaw the end of the Cold War, the fall of the **Berlin Wall** and the end of communism in the USSR. Gorbachev recognised that communism in the USSR faced many problems. For example, the economy was not nearly as efficient as the American economy. While most Americans in the 1980s enjoyed a high standard of living, everyday life in the Soviet Union was dominated by shortages. This, in turn, meant that many Soviet people had lost faith in communism.

Gorbachev introduced three important strategies which greatly changed relationships with the West, and more especially the USA.

● He initiated sweeping reforms in the Communist Party and Soviet system in the USSR. These included *perestroika* (restructuring) which meant economic reforms designed to make the Soviet economy more efficient, and *glasnost* (openness) in which censorship of the press was relaxed.

Source A From an article in *The Sunday Times*, 27 December 1987. The article was discussing Gorbachev's impact on the Soviet Union and the world

The Soviet Union is different thanks to Gorbachev. In the world beyond the Soviet Union he has been the prime instigator of change. At home the changes are remarkable. Compared with just one year ago, Soviet citizens can now think more freely without fear of reprisal. They can emigrate in increasing numbers. Seeing and reading certain plays, films and novels which were once banned is now no longer considered dangerous. Nevertheless, some foreign stations are still jammed and there are still political prisoners.

● He ended the arms race with the USA and signed various arms reduction agreements.
● He stopped Soviet interference in eastern European satellite states such as Poland and Czechoslovakia.

At first Reagan reacted in a negative way towards Gorbachev's reforms. He actually made Gorbachev's reforms much more difficult by doing things like giving speeches demanding the General Secretary 'tear down this wall'. However, eventually Reagan supported the reforms but refused to 'reward' Gorbachev with economic concessions, believing these might encourage the Soviet Union to revive.

Gorbachev wanted to maintain the Soviet Union's role of superpower. He knew that he had to win over the Soviet people and show the world that he would not threaten world peace. He had to be all things to all people. He assumed that *perestroika* and *glasnost* would strengthen the power of the Soviet Communist Party. However, *glasnost* was a two-edged sword for Gorbachev. The more freedom that people gained, the more they wanted and the more they began to criticise Gorbachev – making it more difficult to maintain the Communist Party in power.

The economy had been damaged by the arms race, the space race, the war in Afghanistan and, above all else, by a system that did not encourage incentive. *Perestroika* did bring some considerable changes and certain aspects of a free economy were introduced. However, these were not fast enough to satisfy many Soviet people or make much difference to their standard of living.

▶ The end of the arms race

Arms limitation talks were renewed after it was clear that Gorbachev was keen to change relations with the West. A summit meeting between Gorbachev and Reagan was held in Geneva over two days in November 1985. Though nothing was decided, the Geneva Accord was set out which committed the two countries to speed up arms talks. Both leaders promised to meet in the near future and it was clear to many observers that the two men had got on well.

Although a second summit meeting at Reykjavik in 1986 failed to reach agreement on arms limitation, a third summit in Washington in December 1987 was more successful with the signing of the Intermediate Nuclear Forces Treaty (INF). This treaty eliminated nuclear and conventional ground-launched ballistic and cruise missiles with ranges of 500–5500 kilometres (300–3400 miles). By the treaty's deadline, 1 June 1991, a total of 2692 of such weapons had been destroyed; 846 by the USA and 1846 by the Soviet Union. Also under the treaty, both nations were allowed to inspect each other's military installations.

The INF Treaty was important because it was the first treaty to reduce the number of nuclear missiles that the superpowers possessed. It therefore went much further than SALT I, which simply limited the growth of Soviet and American stockpiles.

After the signing of the INF Treaty, the final summit meeting was held in Moscow in May 1988. Much of the West seemed to be overtaken by what became known as 'Gorbymania'. It was as if Gorbachev had become a pop star. Furthermore, it was evident that the wives of Gorbachev and Reagan had played a part in pushing the two leaders together.

Source B From *Memoirs of Mikhail Gorbachev*, written in 1995. Here he was discussing why the Soviet Union wanted to improve relations with the USA

I realised that it was vitally important to correct the distorted ideas that the Soviet Union had about other nations. These misconceptions had made us oppose the rest of the world for many decades. We understood that in a world of mutual interdependence, progress was unthinkable for any society which was fenced off from the world by impenetrable state frontiers and ideological barriers. We knew that in a nuclear age we could not build a safe security system just based on military means. This prompted us to propose an entirely new idea of global security, which could include all aspects on international relations.

Source C Photograph of President Reagan (centre) and General Secretary Gorbachev (left) signing the INF Treaty at the White House on 8 December 1987

Source D Raisa Gorbachev and Nancy Reagan at the White House, Washington DC

At the Moscow summit there were more arms control talks. The summit led to the Conventional Forces in Europe Treaty (CFE) which was signed by NATO and Warsaw Pact representatives in November 1990. The agreement reduced the number of tanks, missiles and aircraft held by the signatory states.

The USA and the Soviet Union continued to enjoy good relations. The new US President, George Bush Sr, and Gorbachev were able to announce that the Cold War was over in a summit in Malta in 1989. When Saddam Hussein invaded Kuwait in 1990 (see page 158) the two Superpowers acted closely and followed the directives of the United Nations. However, Gorbachev did not commit any troops to the Coalition Forces that invaded Iraq.

At the Washington summit of 31 May–3 June 1990, Bush and Gorbachev discussed Strategic Arms Limitation (START) and finally signed the Treaty for the Reduction and Limitation of Strategic Arms (START 1), on 31 July 1991. It called for both sides to reduce their strategic nuclear arms over the next seven years. This meant reducing 25 to 35 per cent of all their strategic warheads. Bush and Gorbachev signed the treaty with pens made of scrapped missiles.

TASKS

1 Describe Gorbachev's new policies in the Soviet Union. (For guidance on how to answer this type of question, see page 144.)

2 What can you learn from Source A (page 151) about the impact of Gorbachev's policies?

3 Devise a suitable headline for Source A (page 151).

4 Look at Sources B and C (on page 152) which are about relations between the USA and the Soviet Union. Explain why relations between the USA and the Soviet Union changed in the years 1985–90. (For guidance on how to answer this type of question, see pages 126–28.)

5 Study Source D. What does it show you about relations between the USA and the Soviet Union in the late 1980s?

6 Put together a timeline to show the key developments in relations between the USA and the Soviet Union in the years 1985–90. You should include on your timeline the summit meetings and arms agreements. Place positive developments above the line and negative developments below. Explain why each was positive or negative.

Why did the Cold War end?

At the Malta Conference in 1989, US President George Bush Snr declared that the Cold War was over. However, it was not until 1991, with the end of communist control of Eastern Europe and the fall of the Soviet Union, that the rivalry between the superpowers really ended.

▶ Changes in Eastern Europe

In December 1988, Gorbachev withdrew Soviet troops from Eastern European bases to save money. In the following year he announced what became known as the Sinatra Doctrine – that members of the **Warsaw Pact**

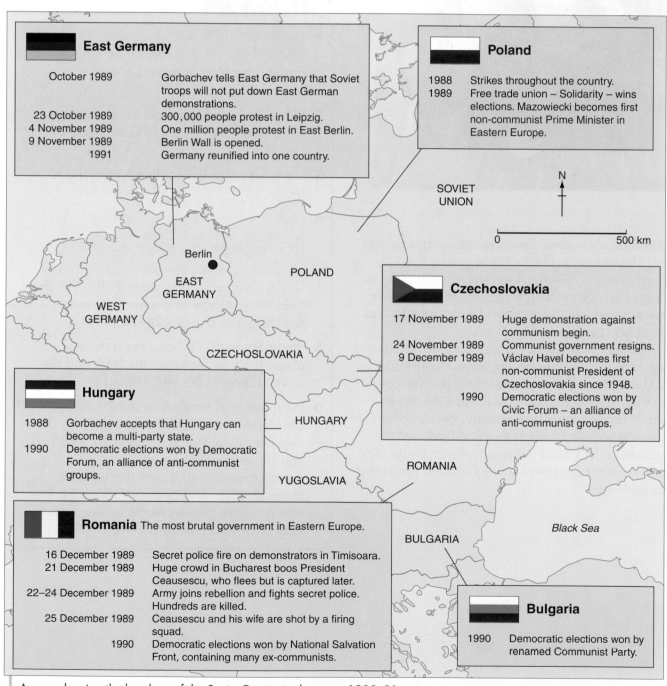

East Germany

October 1989	Gorbachev tells East Germany that Soviet troops will not put down East German demonstrations.
23 October 1989	300,000 people protest in Leipzig.
4 November 1989	One million people protest in East Berlin.
9 November 1989	Berlin Wall is opened.
1991	Germany reunified into one country.

Poland

1988	Strikes throughout the country.
1989	Free trade union – Solidarity – wins elections. Mazowiecki becomes first non-communist Prime Minister in Eastern Europe.

SOVIET UNION

N

0   500 km

Berlin

POLAND

EAST GERMANY

WEST GERMANY

CZECHOSLOVAKIA

Czechoslovakia

17 November 1989	Huge demonstration against communism begin.
24 November 1989	Communist government resigns.
9 December 1989	Václav Havel becomes first non-communist President of Czechoslovakia since 1948.
1990	Democratic elections won by Civic Forum – an alliance of anti-communist groups.

Hungary

1988	Gorbachev accepts that Hungary can become a multi-party state.
1990	Democratic elections won by Democratic Forum, an alliance of anti-communist groups.

HUNGARY

ROMANIA

YUGOSLAVIA

Romania The most brutal government in Eastern Europe.

16 December 1989	Secret police fire on demonstrators in Timisoara.
21 December 1989	Huge crowd in Bucharest boos President Ceausescu, who flees but is captured later.
22–24 December 1989	Army joins rebellion and fights secret police. Hundreds are killed.
25 December 1989	Ceausescu and his wife are shot by a firing squad.
1990	Democratic elections won by National Salvation Front, containing many ex-communists.

Black Sea

BULGARIA

Bulgaria

1990	Democratic elections won by renamed Communist Party.

A map showing the break-up of the Soviet Empire in the years 1988–91

could make changes to their countries without expecting outside interference. He hoped to strengthen communism in Eastern Europe but all he did was weaken it. Once reform had started in these countries, he was unable to contain it.

▶ The fall of the Berlin Wall

This event has come to symbolise the end of the Cold War. However, it would be wrong to confuse the fall of the wall with the end of the war. On 9 November 1989, the East German government announced the opening of the border crossings into West Germany. The people began to dismantle the Berlin Wall. Within a few days, over 1 million people had seized the chance to see relatives and experience life in West Germany. West and East Germany were formally reunited in October 1990.

Tension in the world seemed to ease by the day while the power of the Soviet Union seemed to be dwindling so quickly. The new Germany joined NATO and, in 1991, the Warsaw Pact was dissolved.

▶ The collapse of the Soviet Union

Events in Eastern Europe had a catastrophic impact on the Soviet Union. The many nationalities and ethnic groups saw how the satellite states had been able to break away from Moscow. In 1990, the Baltic states of Estonia, Latvia and Lithuania declared themselves independent, which was accepted by Moscow in 1991. This led to other demands for independence within the Soviet Union.

Gorbachev found that he was opposed by most sections of Soviet society. In August 1991, there was an attempted *coup d'etat* which was defeated by Boris Yeltsin who was President of the Russian Socialist Republic. Gorbachev was restored as General Secretary but he had lost his authority. Gorbachev resigned in December 1991 and the Soviet Union split into several independent states (see map below). Now there was only one superpower left – the USA.

TASKS

1 Construct a flow chart to show how the Soviet Union fell apart (begin and end as follows):

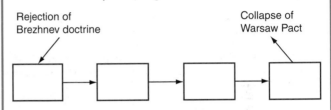

2 Why was the fall of the Berlin Wall so significant?

3 Explain why the USA welcomed the changes that took place in Eastern Europe after 1988.

4 Describe the collapse of the Soviet Union. (For guidance on how to answer this type of question, see page 144.)

5 Was the leadership of Gorbachev a turning point in the Cold War? (For guidance on how to answer this type of question, see pages 75–76.)

A map showing the break-up of the Soviet Union into the Commonwealth of Independent States

What were the key features of US involvement in Iran, Iraq and the Gulf War?

The USA became increasingly involved in the Middle East in the last quarter of the twentieth century, most especially in Iran and Iraq.

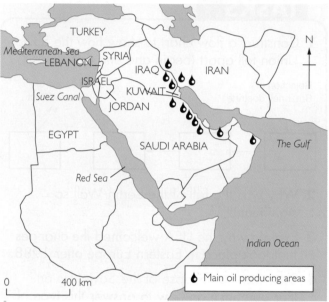

A map of the Middle East showing the main oil producing areas

▶ Iran

America's closest ally in the Persian Gulf region was Mohammed Reza Pahlavi, the Shah of Iran. For 25 years the Shah had tried to modernise Iran by rapid industrialisation and the emancipation of women. However, this modernisation and his increasingly tyrannical government led to his forced abdication in January 1979. This unsettled the whole region.

- The USA had vital oil interests in the Gulf area and especially Iran.
- This period saw the growth of religious fundamentalism in the region which demanded an end to Western (more especially American) imperialism and seriously threatened US Middle Eastern oil interests.
- Iran was now controlled by the **fundamentalist** religious leader Ayatollah Ruhollah Khomeini, who denounced the USA as the 'Great Satan' and

announced an Islamic republic determined to destroy all western influences.

The Iranian hostages

On 4 November 1979, the US Embassy in Tehran was taken over by **militant** Iranian students. Sixty-six Americans, including diplomats and their guards, were taken hostage. In return for the release of the hostages, the Ayatollah Khomeini demanded that the United States agree to the **extradition** of the former Shah who was undergoing medical treatment in New York. The crisis dragged on for over a year:

- The US government refused to hand over the Shah and suspended Iranian oil imports. Carter threatened Iran with military action if the hostages were not released.
- The Ayatollah refused to budge and threatened to try some of the hostages on a charge of spying on Iran for the USA.
- In April 1980, a rescue mission by US forces went horribly wrong in the Iranian desert. A helicopter and a refuelling aircraft collided in a staging area. Eight servicemen were killed and the operation was called off.
- Carter lost even more popularity because of his failure to secure the release of the hostages as well as the botched rescue attempt.

Source A From an interview in 2004 with Ebrahim Asgharzadeh, one of the organisers of the seizure of the US Embassy in Tehran, 4 November 1979

We neither thought of the aspects of this move, nor its implications. We only intended to make the world hear our protest. Our only concern was that this move would be opposed by the Revolution's leader, but when we took over the embassy, everything changed within a few hours. The leader supported us and many groups of people came to the embassy to express their support, in a way that the future events went out of our control.

We had no choice but to stay in the embassy and to take care of its staff.

Source B Iranian students massing outside the US Embassy in Tehran

Negotiations for the release of the hostages resumed after the death of the Shah in July 1980. On 20 January 1981, twenty minutes after Reagan was sworn in as President, 52 American hostages were released by Iran into US custody, having spent 444 days in captivity.

TASKS

1 What information can you obtain from Source B about the seizure of the US Embassy in Tehran in 1979?

2 Working in pairs, put together two different captions for Source B:

- one for a US newspaper
- the other for an Iranian newspaper.

3 Look at Sources A and B about events in Tehran in 1979. Explain why relations between the USA and Iran changed after 1979. (For guidance on how to answer this type of question, see pages 126–28.)

The Gulf War, 1990–91

On 2 August 1990 Saddam Hussein, the leader of Iraq, ordered the invasion of Kuwait, one of the leading oil producing countries in the Middle East. In less than 24 hours the country was under Iraqi control. Saddam invaded for several reasons:

- Burdened with debts from Iraq's war with Iran, Saddam saw Kuwait as a rich prize.
- Saddam claimed that Kuwait was historically part of Iraq, although in fact Kuwait had existed as a separate territory since 1899.
- Saddam did not expect the USA to use its military power in support of Kuwait. After all, the USA had been supporting him all the way through the war with the Iranian regime. He believed that the USA valued him as a stabilising influence within the region and in Iraq itself. They had taken no action against him when, in 1988, he brutally crushed a rebellion of the **Kurds** in the north of Iraq.

President Bush Snr took the lead in pressing for action to remove the Iraqis from Kuwait. He used the argument that it was an act of blatant aggression against a smaller neighbouring country. In reality, Bush wanted to protect US economic interests, especially oil interests, in the area.

Source C From George Bush Snr's address to Congress, 11 September 1990

So tonight, I want to talk to you about what's at stake – what we must do together to defend civilized values around the world and maintain our economic strength at home.

Our objectives in the Persian Gulf are clear, our goals defined and familiar: Iraq must withdraw from Kuwait completely, immediately, and without condition. [Applause.] Kuwait's legitimate government must be restored. The security and stability of the Persian Gulf must be assured. And American citizens abroad must be protected. [Applause.]

The United Nations imposed tough sanctions on Iraq and then the USA, Britain and other states sent forces to Saudi Arabia. This was called Operation Desert Shield, designed to defend Saudi Arabia and its vast oil resources from possible Iraqi attack as well as push Iraq out of Kuwait. In November 1990, the USA and its allies vastly increased their forces in the area.

Source D US forces in Kuwait, 1991

With almost 2,000 aircraft, General Norman Schwartkopf, the US commander of the **coalition forces** in the Gulf, opened the campaign with an air assault. Operation Desert Storm, the air offensive against Iraq, was launched on 16 January 1991. In the first ten hours a combination of stealth aircraft, cruise missiles, electronic warfare and precision-guided munitions took apart Iraq's military infrastructure and wrecked its ground forces.

After more than a month of 'softening up', Operation Desert Saber, the ground offensive to liberate Kuwait, was launched on 23 February 1991. By 27 February, Kuwait City had been taken by coalition troops and the following day the US ordered a ceasefire.

Results of the war

Saddam was allowed to withdraw with much of his army intact. The retreating Iraqis were at the mercy of the Allies, but Bush called a ceasefire because:

- he was afraid that if the slaughter continued, the allies would lose the support of the other Arab nations
- it was widely expected outside Iraq that after his humiliating defeat, Saddam Hussein would soon be overthrown.

When the Gulf War ended in the defeat of Saddam, Bush's reputation stood high. However, as time passed, he was increasingly criticised for not having pressed home the advantage and for allowing the brutal Saddam to remain in power. Saddam not only survived but had enough troops, tanks and aircraft to brutally suppress rebellions by Shia Muslims in the south and the Kurds in the north.

▶ Developments in foreign policy – conclusion

American foreign policy had undergone significant changes in the last twenty years of the twentieth century. Détente under Carter gave way to the 'second Cold War' under Reagan. However, Gorbachev's reforms brought an end to the Cold War. The US became increasingly involved in the Middle East with the emergence of Islamic fundamentalism in Iran and the ambitions of the Iraqi dictator Saddam Hussein.

TASKS

4 Explain why relations between the USA and Iraq changed between 1980 and 1991. (You may wish to use Source C for information.)

5 Study Source D. What does it show you about US foreign policy in the Middle East?

6 Put together a mind map to summarise the key features of the first Gulf War. Your mind map should include reasons for Saddam's invasion of Kuwait, US and world reactions, the defeat of Iraq and the results of the war.

7 What have been the most important factors in bringing about change in the USA's role in world affairs in the years 1979–2000? In your answer you may wish to discuss the following:

- Reagan and Gorbachev
- the end of the Cold War
- the Iranian hostages
- the first Gulf War

and any other relevant factors.

(For guidance on how to answer this type of question, see pages 108–10.)

Examination practice

Here is an opportunity for you to practise two more questions similar to those that may appear in Section A, and three questions similar to those that may appear in Section B. The questions cover all the types of questions that may appear on the Unit 3 examination paper. See page 22 for Question 1.

You are required to answer **two** questions from Section A and **one** question from Section B.

Question 2: This question is about Changing Attitudes to the Race Issue in the USA, 1930–2000

(a) Describe the role and activities of the Black Power movement. **(5 marks)**
- You will need to describe at least three key features.
- Be specific, avoid generalised comments.
- For further guidance, see pages 41–42.

(b) Look at these two sources about public transport in the USA and answer the question that follows.

Source A From a GCSE history examination paper

In most states in the southern USA, segregation was a fact of life. One aspect of life which was clearly segregated was public transport. Buses, trains and waiting rooms all had areas for black and white people.

Source B A black American speaking in 1961

This was to be my first freedom ride. I entered the white waiting room to wait for the bus. I approached the refreshment counter. I was pushed outside into an alleyway and six men started swinging at me with fists and sticks. Within seconds I was unconscious.

Explain how far the treatment of black people on public transport had changed by the early 1960s. **(7 marks)**

[In your answer you should use the information in the sources and your own knowledge to show the extent of change and the reasons for this.]

- You must make direct reference to the content of each source, describing and expanding upon the key points, showing the change that took place.
- Provide context by bringing in your own knowledge of this topic area, highlighting the changes and, if necessary, the reasons for those changes.
- For further guidance, see pages 60–62.

(c) Why was the Second World War a turning point in the growth of the Civil Rights movement? **(8 marks)**
- You must evaluate the importance or significance of the named individual, event or issue.
- Make reference to the key word in the question – importance, significance or turning point.
- The question requires you to make a judgement and to support it with specific factual detail.
- For further guidance, see pages 75–76.

Question 3: This question is about the USA and the Wider World, 1930–2000

(a) Describe the main developments during the Berlin Airlift. **(5 marks)**
- You will need to describe at least three key features.
- Be specific, avoid generalised comments.
- For further guidance, see page 144.

(b) Look at these two sources about American foreign policy and answer the question that follows.

Source A An American politician speaking in 1935

There will be no opposition to any action which our government takes to bring about world peace as long as it does not commit 130 million American people to another world war. I fear we are again being expected to police the world and sort out Europe's problems. We do not want to get involved in Europe.

Source B From a school history text book

America's policy of isolationism was over by the 1940s. In 1947 the USA issued the Truman Doctrine, a policy of 'containment' to prevent countries from becoming communist.

Explain why American foreign policy had changed up to the late 1940s. (7 marks)

[In your answer you should use the information in the sources and your own knowledge to show the extent of change and the reasons for this.]
- You must make direct reference to the content of each source, describing and expanding upon the key points, showing the change that took place.
- Provide context by bringing in your own knowledge of this topic area, highlighting the changes and, if necessary, the reasons for those changes.
- For further guidance, see pages 126–28.

(c) Why was the Cuban Missile Crisis a turning point in American foreign policy? (8 marks)
- You must evaluate the importance or significance of the named individual, event or issue.
- Make reference to the key word in the question – importance, significance or turning point.
- The question requires you to make a judgement and to support it with specific factual detail.
- For further guidance, see pages 75–76.

Section B: Answer **one** question only from this section
Marks for spelling, punctuation and the accurate use of grammar are allocated to this question. (3)

Question 4

What have been the most important developments that have changed life in America since 1930?
(12 marks)

In your answer you may wish to discuss the following:

- the effects of the Depression
- the impact of World War II
- the policies of the American presidents since 1970
and any other relevant factors.

Question 5

What have been the most important factors in bringing about change in the lives of black Americans since 1930? (12 marks)

In your answer you may wish to discuss the following:

- the impact of World War II
- the Civil Rights movements
- progress made by black Americans by the end of the twentieth century
and any other relevant factors.

Question 6

How far has the USA's role in world affairs changed since 1930? (12 marks)

In your answer you may wish to discuss the following:

- the policy of isolationism
- the impact of World War II
- the USA and the Cold War
and any other relevant factors.

In the essay question you must aim to:
- Make sure you cover the whole period, 1930–2000, and avoid concentrating too much on one narrow time span such as the Second World War era or the decade of the 1960s.
- Use the information provided in the scaffold to help you discuss key periods of change/development, and use your own knowledge to include other periods of significant change/development.
- Remember the rules of essay writing – introduction, several paragraphs of discussion, and a reasoned conclusion.
- For further guidance, see pages 108–10.

GLOSSARY

Air corridor An air route along which aircraft are allowed to fly

Allied powers Countries fighting on the same side during the Second World War

American Civil War A war fought between the southern states (Confederacy) and the northern States, 1861–65

Anti-hero Central character in a film who lacks the qualities of a normal hero

Baby boom Temporary marked increase in the birth rate

Balance the budget Ensure government spending matches revenue

Battle of the Bulge Nickname for the Second Battle of the Ardennes, December 1944

Beatniks Members of the Beat Generation

Berlin Wall Wall built by the East Germans in 1961 to separate East and West Berlin

Blockade The surrounding or blocking of a place

Bolshevik revolution The seizure of power by the Bolsheviks (communists) in Russia in October 1917

Bonds A certificate issued by the government promising to repay borrowed money

Brains trust Later known as brain trust, this began as a term for a group of close advisors to a political candidate or incumbent, prized for their expertise in particular fields. The term is most associated with the group of advisors to Franklin Roosevelt during his presidential administration. More recently the use of the term has expanded to encompass any group of advisers to a decision maker, whether or not in politics

Brinkmanship The policy of pushing a dangerous situation to the brink of disaster

Budget deficit Over-spending

Capitalism Private ownership of the means of production

Cash and carry Following changes to the Neutrality Act, countries at war could buy war material from the USA as long as they arranged for the transport using their own ships and paid immediately in cash

Civil rights The rights of a citizen to social and political equality

Civil rights movement The movement in the USA for equal rights for black citizens

Coalition forces The countries who fought against Saddam Hussein during the first Gulf War

Cold War State of hostility between the USA and the USSR without actually fighting

Collective bargaining Negotiation between workers, represented by union leaders, and employers

Communism A political theory which advocates that all means of production should be owned by the state and each is paid according to his or her needs and abilities

Congress The parliament of the USA divided into the Senate and the House of Representatives

Conscription A law requiring all men or women of a certain age to join the armed forces

Constitutional Actions which follow the constitutional system of government

Containment The actions of the US government to prevent communism spreading to other countries

CORE The Congress of Racial Equality, founded in 1942 to campaign for black civil rights

Counterculture A way of life opposed to that which is regarded as normal

Coup d'etat An armed revolution or uprising against an existing government

Defoliants Chemicals sprayed on plants to remove their leaves. They were used by the US military to destroy the jungles of South Vietnam during the Vietnam War

Democrat Supporter or member of the more reforming political party of the USA, the Democratic Party

Détente An easing of strained relations

Direct action Actions such as strikes or sit-ins

Disenfranchised the loss of the right to vote

Dixiecrat Member of the Democratic Party who opposed civil rights for black Americans

Domino Theory The belief that if one state fell to communism it would be quickly followed by neighbouring states

Drive-in cinema A cinema where films could be watched while sitting in your car

Extradition The official process whereby one nation or state surrenders a suspected or convicted criminal

FBI The Federal Bureau of Investigation, set up to investigate organised crime

Feminist Supporter of women's rights who believes that men and women are equal in all areas

Feminist movement Movement set up to campaign for equal rights for women

Fifth Amendment An amendment to the Constitution of the United States that imposes restrictions on the government's prosecution of persons accused of crimes

Fireside chat Radio talks given by President Roosevelt to keep up the morale of the American people

Freedom marches Marches organised by Martin Luther King and others to campaign for civil rights

Freedom rides These were taken by civil rights activists who rode interstate buses into the segregated southern United States to test the United States Supreme Court

Fundamentalist Someone who adheres strictly to the beliefs of a particular religion

General Motors A leading manufacturer of cars

Generation gap Difference in outlook and beliefs between members of two different generations

Great Depression The economic and social slump which followed the Wall Street Crash of 1929

Great Society The name given by President Johnson to his reforming programme of the 1960s

Guerrilla A member of an irregular armed force that fights a stronger force by sabotage and harassment

Hobo An unemployed wanderer seeking work

Hollywood Ten The name given to ten leading film producers, directors and writers who were accused of being communist in 1947

Hooverville Shanty towns built on the edge of American cities by the unemployed during the early years of the Great Depression

House of Representatives The lower house of the US Congress

Impeachment To bring to trial for treason the president of the USA

Import duties Taxes on goods coming into the country

Indirect taxes A tax, such as a sales tax or value-added tax, that is levied on goods or services rather than individuals

Industrialist Someone who owns and/or runs a business

Infant mortality rate The number of deaths in the first year of life per 1000 children born

Irangate Nickname given to a US political scandal in 1987 involving senior members of the Reagan administration

Iron Curtain Imaginary barrier to the passage of people and information between Soviet-controlled Eastern Europe and the West

Isolationism The policy of holding aloof from the affairs of other countries

Ku Klux Klan Or KKK; a racist secret society of white people in the USA

Kurds An Iranian-speaking group who have historically inhabited the mountainous areas to the south of the Caucasus

Labour unions Trade unions in the USA

Laissez-faire The belief that people should help themselves rather than be helped by the state

League of Nations An international organisation set up in 1920 to try to maintain world peace

Linkage Name given to Nixon's attempts to make links between various foreign policies, especially in Vietnam

Lynching The illegal execution, usually by hanging, of an accused person by a mob

Male supremacy The belief that society should be controlled by men

Method actors The name given to a genre of film actors who tried to think exactly like the character they were portraying

Montgomery Improvement Agency Or MIA; organisation set up to organise the Montgomery bus boycott

Migrate Move from one place to another

Militant Someone who holds extreme views and is prepared to use extreme, even violent, methods

Militant Islam Followers of Islam prepared to use extreme methods

Minimum wage The lowest legal wage per hour that someone can be paid

Multiplex movie theatre This is a cinema complex with more than three screens for viewing

Munitions Weapons of war

National Association for the Advancement of Colored People Or NAACP; organisation set up in 1909 to campaign for civil rights

National debt Money owed by the government

NATO North Atlantic Treaty Organisation set up in 1949, a defensive alliance of countries dominated by the USA

New Deal The name given to the policies of President Franklin Roosevelt to deal with the effects of the Great Depression

New Frontier The name given to the reform policies of President Kennedy in the early 1960s

Peonage A system in which a debtor must work for a creditor until the debt is paid off

Poll taxes A tax that was introduced in certain US states. This tax had to be paid before the person qualified for the vote

Reaganomics The nickname given to the economic policies of President Reagan

Recession This means a general slow-down in economic growth

Red Army The name given to the armed forces of the Soviet Union

Red Scare The name given to the growing fear of communism in the USA, especially in the years after the Second World War

Relief agencies Organisations set up to help the poor and unemployed. More commonly associated with the New Deal, although Herbert Hoover also implemented some

Reparations Compensation paid to victorious countries for damage caused by defeated nations

Republican A member of one of the USA's more conservative political parties, the Republican Party

Rugged individualism The American ideal that individuals are responsible for their own lives without help from anyone else, especially the government

Second front This was the idea of an Anglo-American invasion of mainland Europe during the Second World War to take pressure off the Soviet Union

Segregation The enforced separation of racial groups in a community

Senate The upper house of the US Congress

Senator A representative from the upper house, the Senate. There are two senators per state

'Separate but equal' This was the legal justification in the USA for segregation, especially in education

Sexual permissiveness Freedom to have relationships outside marriage, often with more than one partner

Sharecropper A participant in a system of agriculture in which a landowner allows a tenant to use the land in return for a share of the crop produced on the land

Sit-ins A form of direct action that involves one or more persons non-violently occupying an area for a protest

Student Non-violent Coordinating Committee Or SNCC; organisation set up in 1960 to campaign for black civil rights

Socialist Someone who believes that society as a whole should own the means of production, distribution and exchange

Southern Christian Leadership Conference Or SCLC; organisation set up in 1957 to campaign for civil rights for black Americans

Soviet Union The Union of Soviet Socialist Republics, informally known as the Soviet Union, set up in 1924 but which broke up in 1991

State Department The federal department in the United States that sets and maintains foreign policies

State government Governments which are locally elected to run state affairs

State of the Union Address An annual address presented by the President of the United States to the United States Congress

Stock market A public market for the buying or selling of company shares

Superpower A term used for the two most powerful countries in the world after 1945 – the USA and the USSR

Supreme Court The highest judicial body in the United States

Totalitarianism A form of government in which the ruler is an absolute dictator

Trade embargo A government banning trade with another country

Trade sanctions One or more trade barriers that a country places upon another country as a punishment

Tupperware party A party organised to sell a range of plastic containers for storing food

United Nations An international organisation set up after the Second World War to try to prevent wars and help under privileged countries

Universal health insurance Health insurance which applies to all the population of a country

USSR Union of Soviet Socialist Republics was the alternative name for the Soviet Union

Vietcong A communist guerrilla force that sought to overthrow the South Vietnamese government

Vietminh The League for the Independence of Vietnam, a nationalist- and communist-dominated movement

Vietnamisation The US government policy of transferring the fighting of the war in Vietnam from the American forces to those of South Vietnam

Wall Street Crash The term used for the collapse of the American stock market in October 1929

Warsaw Pact A military alliance set up in 1955 which included the Soviet Union and Eastern European states

White supremacy The idea that white Americans should control US society

Youth culture The beliefs, attitudes and interests of teenagers

INDEX